The Great
AMERICAN
SAMPLER
COOKBOOK

The Great AMERICAN SAMPLER COOKBOOK

RECIPES from the WHITE HOUSE & CONGRESS

LINDA BAUER

TAYLOR TRADE PUBLISHING

Lanham • New York • Dallas • Boulder • Toronto • Oxford

Published by Taylor Trade Publishing
An imprint of The Rowman & Littlefield Publishing Group, Inc.
4501 Forbes Boulevard, Suite 200
Lanham, Maryland 20706

Distributed by National Book Network

Library of Congress Cataloging-in-Publication Data

Bauer, Linda.
    Great American sampler cookbook : recipes from the White House and Congress / Linda Bauer.
        p. cm.
    Includes index.
    ISBN 1-58979-131-2 (paper : alk. paper) 1. Cookery, American. I. Title.
TX715.B34922 2004
641.5973—dc22   2004002539

♾™ The paper used in this publication meets the minimum requirements of American National Standard for Information Sciences—Permanence of Paper for Printed Library Materials, ANSI/NISO Z39.48–1992.
Manufactured in the United States of America.

To my husband, Steve, a fellow writer, an avid reader, and my best friend. To our sons, Michael and Chris, who learned about the joy of reading at the age of three. May this book provide the impetus for others to also share in that pleasure and hopefully change lives.

To my mother who passed away over ten years ago. Her unselfish dedication to others is still an inspiration for us each day. She was a strong proponent of phonics, simply because she learned by sight reading and experienced difficulty with that method. She was so happy that her daughter and grandsons learned using phonics and were enthusiastic readers.

To Rick Rinehart of The Rowman & Littlefield Publishing Group. It is a joy once again to work with you. Your commitment to literacy is encouraging and your professionalism is refreshing.

To Barbara Bush for her inspiration because she believes that the home is a child's first school, the parent is a child's first teacher, and reading is a child's first subject. She also supports the development of family literacy programs where children and parents read together.

Laura Bush's love of reading is evident in her duties as First Lady, in her support for teachers and librarians, and in her own fight for literacy. She extols the love of books—of holding a book, turning its pages, looking at the pictures, and hearing wonderful stories read aloud—as key to developing a love of learning and to building important skills.

To all of America's teachers, tutors, parents, and literacy volunteers who endeavor to share their love of reading with others.

Contents

★

Foreword

★

The Great American Sampler Cookbook started as a literal dream to fight world hunger. It became a reality with the help of then Senator Metzenbaum and then Congressman John Kasich of Ohio and President and Mrs. Ronald Reagan. The kind cooperation of dedicated statesmen and their families created a beautiful book that helped the Red Cross in their endeavors.

The second version of the book was written during the presidency of George H. W. Bush. A collection was created that aided World Vision to establish programs worldwide to help bring water and food to those in need.

This third effort, *The Great American Sampler Cookbook*, fulfills a cause that I fervently share with Barbara and Laura Bush—stamping out illiteracy. If such a task is accomplished, just imagine how many other problems could be solved at the same time. Thank you for supporting this dream. Hopefully your family will enjoy many of the more than two hundred recipes from our statesmen. They represent food from every corner of America. The love of great food and the bounty of our nation are evident in each and every recipe. Many contributors chose to tell of their ethnic backgrounds, favorite indigenous foods, and fond memories of meals shared with others. Enjoy, and may God continue to bless America!

Acknowledgments

★

Special thanks to President and Mrs. Bush, Vice President and Mrs. Cheney, members of Congress, and their families for their extremely generous contributions to this book. Their dedication to the fight for literacy is most encouraging and steadfast.

All of the proceeds from this book will go directly to further the cause of literacy in America.

APPETIZERS

★ 1

Dips, Pates,
Hors d'oeuvres,
and First Courses

PRESIDENT'S GUACAMOLE

President George W. Bush

4 ripe avocados (preferably Haas)
2 jalapenos, seeded and diced
1 lime, juiced
1 clove garlic, finely minced
2 medium vine-ripened tomatoes, seeded and diced
1 medium yellow onion, diced
¼ cup cilantro leaves, washed, dried, and finely chopped
Kosher salt to taste
Freshly ground pepper to taste

Halve and pit avocados and scoop flesh into a bowl. Mash avocado to desired consistency. Using rubber gloves, seed and dice jalapenos.

Mix in remaining ingredients. Cover with plastic wrap and refrigerate for about an hour before serving.

Serve with tortilla chips.

CRAB PATE

Representative Jim Turner, TEXAS

1 10½-ounce can cream of mushroom soup, undiluted
1 envelope gelatin
3 tablespoons cold water
¾ cup real mayonnaise
1 8-ounce package cream cheese, softened
1 can white crabmeat, drained and flaked
1 small onion, grated
1 cup celery, finely chopped
Fresh parsley for garnish

Heat soup in saucepan until warm. Dissolve gelatin in water; add to soup, stirring well. Add remaining ingredients, mixing well.

Spoon into oiled 4-cup mold or loaf pan. Chill until firm. (Best made the day before.)

Unmold, garnish with parsley, and serve with crackers.

Serve at your next party—it's delicious!

HOT CHICKEN WINGS
A LA THOMAS

Senator Craig Thomas, WYOMING

1   pound chicken wings
1   tablespoon butter
1 or 2   4½-ounce bottles Durkee Red Hot sauce

Cut off and discard wingtips. Set oven to 400 degrees. Put wings on rack or broiler pan and cook for 30 minutes.

Meanwhile, melt butter over low heat in a saucepan. Add Durkee Red Hot sauce. Heat until thoroughly mixed.

After the wings are cooked to a crisp, put into the hot sauce mix and coat thoroughly.

Right before serving, put wings on broiler pan and broil for 30 seconds to crisp the topping.

Serve with lots of napkins and water! Enjoy!

MARGE'S CHILE CON QUESO DIP

Representative Tom Udall, NEW MEXICO

1	pound cubed Swiss cheese
32	ounces tomato sauce
8 to 10	roasted and diced hot green chilies
2	tablespoons garlic salt

Mix all ingredients together in a saucepan over low heat. If mixture appears too thick, add a little more tomato sauce. DO NOT mix a lot; stir occasionally.

When completely melted, eat like a dip with plain tortilla chips.

A New Mexico classic loved by everyone. Buen provecho.

GUACAMOLE

Representative Tom DeLay, TEXAS

4 well-ripened avocados, peeled and diced
2 tomatoes, peeled and diced
1 medium onion, very finely chopped
  Salt to taste
  Pepper to taste
  Garlic salt to taste
1 tablespoon lemon juice

Combine avocados, tomatoes, and onion in a bowl. Add salt, pepper, and garlic salt. By hand, mash all ingredients together until smooth.

Do not blend with electric blender or mixer. Lightly sprinkle dip with lemon juice to prevent discoloration.

Serve dip along with tortilla or corn chips.

BIG BEND BEAN DIP

★

Representative Tom DeLay, TEXAS

2 cups cooked pinto beans
1 small onion, chopped
2 tablespoons bacon drippings or butter
⅓ cup sharp cheddar cheese, grated
4 ounces jalapeno peppers, drained, seeded, and chopped
Salt to taste
Pepper to taste

Mash beans until quite smooth, or blend in blender. Set aside. Saute onion in bacon drippings or butter until soft. Add beans and remaining ingredients to onion and stir over low heat until cheese melts. Serve warm with corn chips or tostada shells.

Makes about 3 cups of dip.

PICNIC PATE

Senator Christopher Bond, MISSOURI

4   tablespoons butter

½   pound fresh mushrooms

4   green onions, minced

4   tablespoons sherry

8   ounces liverwurst

2   8-ounce packages cream cheese, softened

1   teaspoon chopped fresh dill

1   teaspoon chopped fresh chervil

2   teaspoons Dijon mustard

Salt to taste

Freshly ground pepper to taste

Melt butter in a skillet. Saute mushrooms and green onions until soft. Stir in sherry.

Cool.

Place mushroom mixture and remaining ingredients in a food processor or blender. Process until very smooth. Transfer to a crock or serving bowl.

Refrigerate for at least 24 hours before serving. Garnish with sprigs of fresh dill. Serve with party rye and a selection of pickles.

Makes 12 servings.

> Mushrooms are the magic in this savory pate. Tuck it away in a picnic basket along with a hefty supply of sandwiches, pickles, and fresh fruit and enjoy an outing under the Gateway Arch.

EASTER EGG DIP

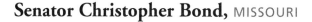

Senator Christopher Bond, MISSOURI

2 tablespoons lemon juice

1 tablespoon onion juice

1 teaspoon coarse ground mustard

2 teaspoons mustard

½ cup mayonnaise

½ teaspoon Tabasco sauce

6 hard-cooked eggs, chopped

½ teaspoon seasoned salt

¼ teaspoon white pepper

4 ounces olive-and-pimento cream cheese, whipped

Fresh parsley or dill, chopped

In a mixer or blender, combine juices, mustards, mayonnaise, and Tabasco sauce. Add eggs one by one, beating after each addition until smooth and light.

Beat in salt, pepper, and cream cheese. Turn into chilled bowl, smooth top, and garnish with chopped fresh parsley or dill. Serve with raw vegetables or assorted crackers. May be spread on bread for tea sandwiches.

Makes 2 cups.

Reviving an old tradition, we hosted our first Easter-egg hunt on the lawn of the Missouri Governor's Mansion in 1973. Since our son Sam arrived, the hunt has become an annual event. This unusual dip proved the perfect solution for leftover Easter eggs.

CURRY CAPER DIP

Senator Christopher Bond, MISSOURI

1 cup mayonnaise

½ cup sour cream

1 teaspoon crushed herbs, such as basil, thyme, or oregano

¼ teaspoon salt

⅛ teaspoon curry

1 tablespoon onion, grated

1 tablespoon fresh parsley, chopped

1½ teaspoons lemon juice

2 teaspoons capers, drained

½ teaspoon Worcestershire sauce

Mix all ingredients. Chill. Serve with crudités (raw vegetables). For a colorful presentation, spoon the dip into a hollowed-out red cabbage or eggplant.

Makes 1½ cups.

My favorite dip for raw vegetables always recalls memories of the good friend who parted with this gem.

MUSTARD SAUCE

Senator Chuck Grassley, IOWA

4   tablespoons dry mustard
1   tablespoon butter
¼   cup water
6   tablespoons sugar
6   tablespoons vinegar
1   beaten egg

Make a paste of the dry mustard, butter, and water. Add sugar and vinegar. Bring to a boil. Add beaten egg.

Cook until thick. Refrigerate. Pour over an 8-ounce block of cream cheese. Serve with crackers.

Makes 20 servings.

We've enjoyed this treat with Sue, a former Des Moines girl. Her backyard adjoins ours.

ITALIAN COPENATA

Representative John Elias Baldacci, MAINE

2 pounds fresh eggplant
1 tablespoon salt
2 cups celery, coarsely chopped
1 cup carrot, chopped
¾ cup yellow onion, chopped
2 tablespoons olive oil
⅓ cup red wine vinegar
4 teaspoons sugar
3 cups canned tomatoes, mashed
2 tablespoons tomato paste
6 green olives, chopped
2 tablespoons capers
5 anchovies in oil
  Salt to taste
  Pepper to taste

Cut eggplant in cubes and dust with salt. Drain in a colander. Use a large frying pan to saute celery, carrot, and onion in olive oil for 15 minutes.

Saute the drained eggplant for 10 minutes in a little oil. Place all of these in a heavy 2-quart kettle and add wine vinegar, sugar, canned tomatoes, tomato paste, green olives, capers, and anchovies. Simmer for 15 to 20 minutes.

Add salt and pepper. Chill and serve.

My family has owned and operated an Italian restaurant in Bangor, Maine, for many years. I grew up working in the restaurant with my brothers and sisters, and I learned the value of hard work and cooperation. I have been fortunate to have been able to put these qualities to good use in my service to Congress.

CHEESE BALL

★

Senator Chuck Grassley, IOWA

2 8-ounce packages cream cheese, softened
1 package Good Seasons Italian salad dressing mix, dry
1 cup pecans, chopped

Mix cream cheese, salad dressing mix, and ½ cup chopped nuts. Shape into two balls and roll in the remaining chopped pecans. Makes 24 servings.

Best if made a little ahead so flavors can blend. Serve with crackers.

FIESTA CHEESE WHEEL

Senator Christopher Bond, MISSOURI

1   14½-ounce can whole plum tomatoes, drained
1   8-ounce package cream cheese, softened
8   ounces cheddar cheese, grated
½   cup butter softened
½   cup onion, finely chopped
2   cloves garlic, crushed
1   teaspoon salt
¼   teaspoon cayenne pepper
⅛   teaspoon ground cumin
¾   cup walnuts, chopped
2   tablespoons fresh parsley, chopped

Seed tomatoes and dry between paper towels. Combine tomatoes, cheese, butter, onion, garlic, salt, cayenne pepper, and cumin. Beat until smooth.

Spoon mixture onto a large piece of waxed paper. Shape into a wheel approximately 1-inch thick. Chill until firm.

Cover wheel with chopped walnuts. Sprinkle with parsley.

Serve as an appetizer with crackers or tortilla chips.

Makes 20 servings.

> Great for a tailgate party before a Cardinals or Chiefs game.

SWEET AND SOUR MEATBALLS

★

Senator Christopher Bond, MISSOURI

MEATBALLS:
- 5 pounds ground chuck
- 1 pound ground pork
- 4 eggs
- 4 teaspoons salt
- 2 teaspoons pepper
- 1 teaspoon nutmeg
- 3 tablespoons seasoning salt
- 4 cups light cream
- 1 large onion, finely chopped
- 12 ounces bread crumbs

SWEET AND SOUR SAUCE:
- 4 13-ounce cans chunked pineapple
- ½ cup cornstarch
- 1 cup red wine vinegar
- 2 cups brown sugar
- ¼ cup soy sauce
- 1 green pepper, finely diced

We were still new-lyweds when Kit ran for the U.S. Congress in 1968, and our first parade of that campaign was during the Hermann Maifest. Following the event, we were invited to a reception where these savory meatballs were served. Featuring pork and soy, two of Missouri's major agricultural products, they are always a popular item on a buffet table.

Combine all meatball ingredients. Shape mixture into balls about 1 inch in diameter. Brown in vegetable oil. Drain, cool, and refrigerate.

For sauce, drain pineapple, retaining juice. Add enough water to juice to make 4 cups. Dissolve cornstarch in vinegar. Combine all ingredients, except green pepper. Cook, stirring constantly, until thickened. Add green pepper. Heat thoroughly. To serve, heat meatballs in sauce. Transfer to a chafing dish.

Makes 9 dozen.

ARTICHOKE DIP

Representative David L. Hobson, OHIO

1   8½-ounce can artichoke hearts
1   cup mayonnaise
1   cup Parmesan cheese, grated
½   lemon, juiced
    Cayenne pepper to taste

Drain, rinse, and mash artichokes. Mix together all ingredients. Turn into small buttered baking dish.

Bake in preheated 350-degree oven for 30 minutes or until bubbly and brown on top. Serve in baking dish on a platter surrounded by favorite crackers.

Makes 2½ cups.

CRABMEAT MOLD

Representative David L. Hobson, OHIO

2 envelopes gelatin

¼ cup water

1 can tomato soup

3 8-ounce packages cream cheese

1 cup mayonnaise

1 small can crabmeat

⅓ cup celery, chopped

⅓ cup onion, chopped

⅓ cup green pepper, chopped

In a large bowl, dissolve gelatin in water. Let stand. Heat soup in double boiler. When hot, add cheese and stir until cheese softens. Cool.

Add mayonnaise, crabmeat, celery, onion, and green pepper. Mix with gelatin. Pour into mold and refrigerate overnight.

Serve with crackers or melba toast.

CRABMEAT SPREAD

Representative David L. Hobson, OHIO

1	8-ounce package cream cheese, softened
1	lemon, juiced
3	tablespoons mayonnaise
1 to 2	teaspoons Worcestershire sauce
1	tablespoon onion, grated
1	teaspoon garlic powder
6	ounces frozen Alaskan king crab, thawed, drained, and shredded
6	ounces chili sauce
2	tablespoons parsley flakes

In a small mixing bowl, beat together all ingredients except crab, chili sauce, and parsley flakes. Beat until smooth. Spread mixture into one or two shallow glass serving dishes.

Spread chili sauce on cream cheese mixture. Top with shredded crabmeat.

Cover and refrigerate for at least 24 hours. Sprinkle with parsley flakes before serving. Serve with crackers or favorite meat.

WILD DUCK PATE

Senator John Breaux, LOUISIANA

GELATIN TOPPING:
- 1 envelope gelatin
- 1 cup beef bouillon
- 1 tablespoon Worcestershire sauce
- ¾ tablespoon lemon juice
- 2 dashes Tabasco sauce

DUCKS:
- 4 mallard ducks
- Salt to taste
- Pepper to taste
- Tony's Creole seasoning
- 2 onions, chopped
- 2 stalks celery, chopped
- 1 green pepper, chopped
- Red wine
- Water

PATE:
- 2 envelopes gelatin
- ¾ cup reserved duck liquor
- 5 hard-cooked eggs, grated
- 2 small onions, grated
- 3 stalks celery, finely chopped
- 1½ cups mayonnaise

Sprinkle gelatin over ¼ cup bouillon and let stand 5 minutes. In the top of a double boiler over hot water, dissolve the gelatin. Add remaining bouillon, Worcestershire sauce, lemon juice, and Tabasco sauce. Spray a 1½-quart mold with cooking spray. Add bouillon mixture and chill until set.

Season ducks with salt, pepper, and Creole seasoning, and rub into skin. Put ducks in roasting pan and cover with onion, celery, and bell pepper. Put a combination of red wine and water in roaster to almost cover the ducks. Cover and bake at 350 degrees for about 2 hours until the ducks are tender. Skin and debone ducks; place meat in bowl or food processor and process until fine. Strain and reserve ¾ cup duck liquor.

Sprinkle gelatin over ¼ cup reserved duck liquor and let stand 5 minutes. In top of a double boiler over hot water, dissolve gelatin. Add duck meat, eggs, celery, and mayonnaise and mix well. Pour over congealed bouillon and chill several hours or overnight to set. Serve with a variety of dark breads.

Makes 30 to 50 servings.

CHEESE WAFERS

Representative Roger Wicker, MISSISSIPPI

8 ounces margarine
2 cups sharp cheddar cheese, grated
2 cups flour
1 dash Tabasco sauce (or more)
1 cup Rice Krispies, crushed

Mix margarine and cheddar cheese by hand. Add flour, Tabasco sauce, and Rice Krispies and continue mixing.

Roll mixture into marble-sized balls. Flatten with fork onto cookie sheet.

Bake at 350 degrees for 15 to 20 minutes. Store in airtight container when cooled. Freeze well.

This recipe is from my mother, Gayle Long. They make a wonderful appetizer as well as a delicious snack. —Gayle Wicker

CHARLESTON EGG BALLS

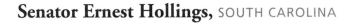

Senator Ernest Hollings, SOUTH CAROLINA

8   hard-cooked eggs, cooled
½   cup butter
1   teaspoon salt
¼   teaspoon red pepper
½   teaspoon Worcestershire sauce
¼   teaspoon celery seed
1   cup bread crumbs

Using an electric mixer or food processor, cream eggs and butter until well blended. Add salt, pepper, Worcestershire sauce, and celery seed. Refrigerate several hours. Form mixture into 1-inch balls, then roll in bread crumbs.

Makes 30 balls.

Since butter is used instead of mayonnaise, there is less chance of spoiling. This was important in the warm climate of Charleston prior to refrigeration and air conditioning.

ALASKA SALMON DIP
A LA LISA

Senator Lisa Murkowski, ALASKA

1   8-ounce package cream cheese, softened
½   cup sour cream
1   tablespoon fresh lemon juice
1   tablespoon fresh dill, minced
1   teaspoon prepared horseradish
½   teaspoon kosher salt
¼   teaspoon freshly ground pepper
4   ounces Alaska salmon, smoked

Cream the cheese until smooth. Add sour cream, lemon juice, dill, horseradish, salt, and pepper. Mix well. Add smoked salmon, mixing well. Chill and serve with crudités (raw vegetables) or crackers.

CRAB PIZZA

Representative Tom Allen, MAINE

1   8-ounce package light cream cheese
1   tablespoon lemon juice
1   tablespoon onion, grated
2   teaspoons Worcestershire sauce
2   tablespoons mayonnaise
4   ounces chili sauce
¼   cup fresh parsley, chopped
6   ounces crabmeat

Blend the first 5 ingredients together. Spread on a round serving plate. Top with chili sauce and refrigerate. Can be made ahead. Just before serving, top with crabmeat and sprinkle with parsley.

Serve with crackers.

OYSTERS ROCKEFELLER

Representative Charlie Norwood, GEORGIA

1   pound bacon, cooked and crumbled
1   cup butter
½   cup flour
1   pint oysters
2   cloves garlic, minced
½   teaspoon salt
¼   teaspoon cayenne pepper
2   packages frozen chopped spinach
    Tabasco sauce
    Parmesan cheese
1   teaspoon anchovy paste

Cook bacon well; drain and crumble. Melt butter in a skillet. Add flour; stir and cook about 5 minutes until well blended. Blend in oyster water, garlic, salt, cayenne pepper and anchovy paste. Place frozen spinach on top of this mixture. Cover and cook over medium heat, stirring every few minutes. Cook until spinach is done, usually about 10 to 15 minutes. This may be prepared ahead and frozen.

Cover cookie sheets with crumpled aluminum foil. Place baking shells on foil. The foil holds the shell in place and makes cleanup easy. Place 1 oyster in each shell. Top with a spoonful of spinach mixture, 3 drops of Tabasco or any hot sauce, and crumbled bacon, then dust with Parmesan cheese. Place in the middle of oven and broil for 8 to 10 minutes, until bubbly.

Serve about three as an appetizer. This can be made into a casserole. Also the spinach is delicious as a vegetable.

We traditionally have this before Thanksgiving and Christmas dinners.

SALADS

★ 2

RASPBERRY BLUEBERRY SALAD

Representative William Goodling, PENNSYLVANIA

6 ounces raspberry gelatin

1 envelope plain gelatin

½ cup cold water

1 cup half-and-half

1 cup sugar

½ teaspoon vanilla

1 8-ounce package cream cheese

½ cup black walnuts

1 cup hot water

21 ounces blueberry pie filling

Layer 1: Dissolve 1 box of raspberry gelatin in a 9- by 13-inch dish according to directions and let set.

Layer 2: Dissolve envelope of plain gelatin in cold water. Heat half-and-half and sugar, then mix in gelatin. Add vanilla and cream cheese and beat well. While warm, add black walnuts. Pour this mixture over the first layer and let set.

Layer 3: Dissolve the remaining box of raspberry gelatin in 1 cup of hot water. Add blueberry pie filling, cool, and pour over second layer.

Makes 24 servings.

HEALTHY COLD
TURKEY SALAD

★

Senator Barbara Boxer, CALIFORNIA

SALAD:

    2   cups cooked white turkey meat, cubed

    ¼ cup sweet red onion, chopped

    ½ cup red or yellow bell pepper, chopped

    ½ cup water chestnuts or jicama, chopped

    ¼ cup walnuts, chopped

       Freshly ground pepper to taste

DRESSING:

    ¼ cup yogurt

    ¼ cup light mayonnaise

    1   teaspoon dill weed

    ¼ cup parsley, minced

       Salt to taste

    1   tablespoon lemon juice

Mix salad ingredients and toss lightly. Combine dressing ingredients and pour over salad. Chill.

Makes 6 servings.

CURRIED CHICKEN SALAD

Senator Christopher Bond, MISSOURI

       2   cups cooked chicken breasts, diced
       4   scallions, sliced
       1   cup water chestnuts, sliced
       2   cups cooked rice, room temperature
       1   cup mayonnaise
       ½   cup prepared chutney
       1   teaspoon curry powder
       1   teaspoon salt
           Freshly ground pepper to taste
       2   bananas
       ¼   cup lemon juice
      1½   cups chopped peanuts

Combine chicken, scallions, and water chestnuts with rice. In a separate bowl, combine mayonnaise, chutney, curry powder, salt, and pepper. Add to chicken and rice mixture. Chill. Taste and adjust seasonings. Cut bananas diagonally into 1-inch slices. Dip slices in lemon juice and coat with peanuts.

To serve, arrange salad on small platter. Surround salad with banana slices and garnish with chopped nuts. Additional condiments may be served: Chopped green peppers, toasted almonds, plumped raisins, and coconut are a few choices.

Makes 6 to 8 servings.

> Following our son Sam's christening at the First Presbyterian Church in my hometown of Mexico, this savory chicken salad was featured along with asparagus and a watermelon basket brimming with fresh fruit. That Father's Day in 1981 is a date we'll never forget.

PASTA SALAD

Senator Richard Lugar, INDIANA

1 pound spaghetti
1 green pepper
1 bunch green onions
2 stalks celery
2 tomatoes
1 cucumber
1 8-ounce bottle Italian dressing
1 bottle McCormick's Salad Supreme

Break spaghetti into bite-sized pieces and cook. Chop vegetables finely. Drain pasta and add all other ingredients. Mix together while pasta is still warm.

Best when made a day ahead and refrigerated. Serve cold or at room temperature.

Makes 15 to 20 servings.

This is an ideal dish for a potluck supper.

SUMMER RICE SALAD

Senator Christopher Bond, MISSOURI

SALAD:

- 3 cups cooked rice, cooled
- ¼ cup mayonnaise
- ½ cup radishes, thinly sliced
- ½ cup scallions, thinly sliced
- 1 sweet red pepper, minced
- 2 tablespoons sweet gherkins, minced
- 1 tablespoon fresh parsley, minced
- 1 tablespoon fresh dill, chopped
- 1 tablespoon fresh chives, snipped

DRESSING:

- ½ cup fresh lemon juice
- 2 teaspoons salt
- 2 garlic cloves, crushed
- 1¼ cups salad oil

Combine salad ingredients and mix well, then set aside. Place lemon juice, salt, and garlic in a food processor or blender and mix well. With machine running, add oil in a thin stream until thoroughly incorporated. (If added too fast, dressing may separate.)

Add dressing to rice mixture and season with salt and pepper. Taste and adjust seasoning.

Refrigerate and allow to return to room temperature before serving. Mound on lettuce leaves and garnish with black olives or red pepper rings.

Makes 8 to 10 servings.

The diversity of Missouri agriculture is possibly most apparent in the Boot Heel. In this southeast corner of the state, you will discover cotton and rice as well as the more typical corn and soybean crops. A barbecue in conjunction with the Sikeston Cotton Carnival yielded this summer sensation.

MARINATED VEGETABLE SALAD

Representative Ike Skelton, MISSOURI

MARINADE:

- ½ cup apple cider vinegar
- ¼ cup sugar
- 1 cup vegetable or olive oil
- 2 cloves garlic, pressed with garlic press or mashed
- ½ cup wine vinegar
- 1 teaspoon dry mustard
- 2 teaspoons salt
- 1 tablespoon dried oregano leaves, crushed
- 1 teaspoon pepper
- 1 8-ounce bottle Italian dressing

VEGETABLES:

- 2 green peppers, thinly sliced
- 1 cucumber, thinly sliced
- 1 head cauliflower, broken into florets
- 6 carrots, thinly sliced
- 1 pound fresh mushrooms, sliced
- 5 stalks celery, sliced
- 1 bunch green onions, sliced
- 1 dozen cherry tomatoes, halved

Bring apple cider vinegar to boil. Add sugar and oil; stir until sugar dissolves. Let mixture cool. Add all remaining marinade ingredients.

Place all prepared vegetables in large noncorrosive bowl or wide-mouthed jar. Pour marinade over vegetables. Cover with plastic wrap.

Refrigerate for 24 hours. Stir or turn mixture at least 3 or 4 times during the 24-hour period. To serve, drain vegetables and place in a clear glass bowl.

Makes 20 servings.

GREEK SALAD

Representative Mike Bilirakis, FLORIDA

DRESSING:

- ½ cup olive oil
- ½ cup wine vinegar
- 1 teaspoon salt
- ¼ teaspoon pepper
- ½ teaspoon sugar
- 1 clove garlic, crushed
- 1 teaspoon dried oregano leaves

SALAD:

- 1 small head lettuce
- 1 medium tomato, sliced
- 1 medium cucumber, sliced
- 3 green onions, chopped
- 1 small green pepper, cut into strips
  Greek black olives
  Greek hot salad peppers (from a jar)
  Feta cheese, cut into cubes or crumbled
  Anchovy fillets, chopped (optional)

Combine all dressing ingredients in a jar or cruet. Shake until thoroughly blended. Prepare well in advance and keep refrigerated until ready to use. Makes 1 cup. Shake well before using.

To prepare salad, break lettuce in small pieces. Place in salad bowl with tomato, cucumber, onion, and green pepper. Top with black olives, hot salad peppers, feta cheese, and anchovy fillets if desired. Pour dressing over salad and serve.

Makes 4 servings.

This is a traditional Greek salad that our family and friends have enjoyed for many years.

SPINACH SALAD AND CALIFORNIA DRESSING

★

Representative David L. Hobson, OHIO

SALAD:

1 to 2 pounds fresh spinach, torn

   1 medium red onion, chopped

   ½ head lettuce, torn

   2 11-ounce cans mandarin oranges, drained

DRESSING:

  1½ cups sugar

   1 teaspoon dry mustard

   1 cup vinegar

   1 teaspoon salt

   2 eggs, beaten frothy

Combine salad ingredients and set aside.

Combine dressing ingredients and bring to a boil for 1 minute. Chill. Toss with salad right before serving.

Makes 10 servings.

ORANGE CHICKEN SALAD

Senator Michael Enzi, WYOMING

SALAD:

6 cups iceberg lettuce, cut in bite-sized pieces

2 11-ounce cans mandarin oranges, drained

3 green onions, sliced thin

¾ cup celery, diced

1 12½-ounce can white chicken, packed in water, drained

¾ cup slivered almonds (optional)

HONEY MUSTARD DRESSING:

¾ cup olive oil

⅓ cup vinegar or lemon juice

6 tablespoons honey

1 teaspoon garlic salt

1 teaspoon dry mustard

½ to 1 teaspoon dill weed

In a large bowl, toss the salad ingredients until well mixed.

Blend dressing ingredients. Add ½ cup dressing to salad.

Toss again. Serve over Chinese noodles.

HANDY DANDY
DIET DRESSING

★

Senator John Breaux, LOUISIANA

6 ounces tomato juice
1 tablespoon Dijon mustard
1 tablespoon lemon juice
2 teaspoons capers
2 egg whites, cooked and chopped
  Garlic powder to taste
  Pepper to taste
3 teaspoons pimento, chopped (optional)

Mix well and chill.
Makes 20 servings.

HOT CHICKEN SALAD

Senator Robert Bennett, UTAH

⅔ cup slivered almonds

4 cups cooked chicken, diced (about 5 breasts)

2 tablespoons lemon juice

¾ cup mayonnaise

2 cups celery, finely chopped

1 cup cream of chicken soup

1 teaspoon onion, minced

1 cup cheddar cheese, grated

1½ cups potato chips or Corn Flakes

Toast almonds on a cookie sheet in a 350-degree oven for 5 to 7 minutes. (Watch carefully.)

Mix all ingredients except cheese and potato chips. Add cheese to top of mixture, followed by chips.

Bake at 400 degrees for 20 minutes.

GUACAMOLE SALAD

★

Representative Tom DeLay, TEXAS

6 avocados, peeled and diced
3 tomatoes, peeled and diced
1 onion, finely chopped
   Salt to taste
   Pepper to taste
1 teaspoon lemon juice

Combine avocados, tomatoes, onion, and seasonings. Mash together by hand. Do not use blender or food processor. Sprinkle top of salad with lemon juice and seal tightly until serving time to prevent discoloration.

Makes 6 servings.

ORIENTAL SPINACH SALAD

★

Senator Bill Frist, TENNESSEE

DRESSING:

- 1 cup oil
- ¼ cup vinegar
- ⅓ cup ketchup
- 2 tablespoons Worcestershire sauce
- ¾ cup sugar
- ½ teaspoon salt
- ¾ cup onion, grated

SALAD:

- 8 ounces fresh spinach
- 8 ounces water chestnuts, sliced
- 8 strips bacon, crumbled
- 3 hard-cooked eggs, chopped

Combine dressing ingredients in a large jar. Shake well and refrigerate overnight. This dressing will stay fresh for 3 weeks. Wash spinach. Toss salad ingredients. Add dressing when ready to serve.

NAPA SALAD

★

Senator Sam Brownback, KANSAS

SALAD:
- 1 head Napa cabbage (Chinese celery)
- 6 green onions
- 2 packages Ramen noodles, flavor packet removed
- 4 ounces slivered almonds
- 4 ounces sunflower seeds, unsalted
- ½ cup butter or margarine

DRESSING:
- 2 tablespoons soy sauce
- 1 cup sugar
- ½ cup tarragon vinegar
- 1 cup sunflower oil

Dice cabbage and onions. Mix together then refrigerate for at least 2 hours. Break apart Ramen noodles. Put noodles, almonds, sunflower seeds, and butter in skillet and saute until slightly brown. Refrigerate. Combine cabbage mixture and noodle mixture 2 hours before serving.

Mix together soy sauce, sugar, vinegar, and oil. Pour over salad 15 minutes before serving. Stir. Serve.

SOUTHWEST POTATO
SALAD FROM OHIO

★

Representative John Boehner, OHIO

10 to 14   red potatoes, washed and unpeeled
2   cups mayonnaise or salad dressing
1   medium ripe tomato, chopped
½   green pepper, chopped
2   green onions, chopped
2   cloves garlic, minced
2   tablespoons fresh cilantro, chopped
1   tablespoon Dijon mustard
2   tablespoons lime juice
1   teaspoon salt
½   teaspoon pepper
½   teaspoon cayenne pepper or more to taste
1   pound bacon, fried and chopped (optional)
    Hard-cooked eggs (optional)

Place potatoes in pot and add cold water to cover by about 2 inches. Bring to a boil and cook for 35 to 40 minutes or until potatoes are done. While potatoes are cooking, combine remaining ingredients in a large bowl. Allow cooked potatoes to cool enough to handle. Cut into sixths or eighths and add to dressing while still warm. Toss gently to coat. Let stand at room temperature for 30 minutes before serving, or refrigerate up to 2 days.

LAYERED SALAD

★

Representative Wally Herger, CALIFORNIA

SALAD:

  1 medium head lettuce
  ½ cup green onions, thinly sliced
  1 cup celery, thinly sliced
  8 ounces water chestnuts, sliced
  10 ounces frozen peas

DRESSING:

  2 cups mayonnaise
  ½ cup Parmesan cheese
  ¼ teaspoon garlic powder

GARNISH:

  3 hard-cooked eggs, grated
  1 pound bacon, cooked and crumbled
  2 or 3 tomatoes, cut in wedges

Layer salad ingredients in the order listed. Top with dressing mixture. Cover and chill up to 24 hours. Garnish before serving.

PRETZEL SALAD

Representative Chet Edwards, TEXAS

1 cup pretzels, crushed
½ cup butter
½ cup sugar
1 8-ounce package cream cheese, softened
1 8-ounce tub whipped topping
½ cup sugar
2 tablespoons cornstarch
¼ cup sugar
20 ounces crushed pineapple, drained, reserving liquid

Mix pretzels, butter, and sugar together and spread into an 8- by 12-inch dish. Bake crust 5 minutes at 350 degrees. Let cool. Mix cream cheese, whipped topping, and sugar. Spread over first layer.

Mix cornstarch, sugar, and pineapple juice drained from the can of crushed pineapple. Cook on stove over medium heat until thick. Let cool. Stir in crushed pineapple.

Spread over second layer. Top with whipped topping. Chill. Serves 12 to 15.

SOUPS AND STEWS

★ 3

Soups,
Chowders,
Stews,
and Chili

BAKED POTATO SOUP

President George W. Bush

1	medium onion, diced
1	large red pepper, diced
2	tablespoons butter or margarine
½	pound bacon, diced, cooked, and drained well
6	cups leftover mashed potatoes
2 to 3	cups whipping cream, half-and-half, or milk
	Kosher salt to taste
	Fresh ground pepper to taste
4	tablespoons sour cream
2	cups sharp cheddar cheese, grated
½	cup chives, minced

In a large soup pot, saute onions and red pepper in butter over medium heat until onions are clear.

Freeze bacon for easier cutting. Add bacon, potatoes, and whipping cream to desired consistency. Skim milk or chicken stock may be used to reduce calories. Salt and pepper to taste.

Serve with a garnish of a dollop of sour cream, grated cheese, and chives.

President George W. Bush

1¼ cups pinto beans

1 teaspoon salt

1 bay leaf

1 teaspoon oregano, dried

1 pound tomatoes, fresh or canned, peeled, seeded, and chopped, juice reserved

2 ancho chilies

1 pound mixed summer squash

4 ears corn (about 2 cups kernels)

2 tablespoons corn or vegetable oil

2 yellow onions, cut into ¼-inch squares

2 cloves garlic, finely chopped

2 tablespoons red chili powder or more to taste

1 teaspoon ground cumin

½ teaspoon ground coriander

8 ounces green beans, cut into 1-inch lengths

4 ounces Monterey Jack or Muenster cheese, grated

½ bunch cilantro leaves, roughly chopped

Whole cilantro leaves for garnish

Soak the beans overnight. Drain. Cook the presoaked beans for about 1½ to 2 hours in plenty of water with the salt, bay leaf, and oregano.

Remove beans from the heat when they are soft but not mushy, as they will continue to cook in the stew. Drain and save the broth. Prepare the tomatoes.

Open the chili pods and remove the seeds and veins. Then cut the chilies into narrow strips. Cut the squash into large pieces. Shave the kernels from the corn.

Heat the oil in a large skillet, and saute the onions over high heat for 1 to 2 minutes. Lower the heat; add the garlic, chili powder, cumin, and coriander and stir everything together. Add a little bean broth so the chili doesn't scorch or burn.

Cook until the onions begin to soften, about 4 minutes, then add the tomatoes and stew for 5 minutes. Stir in the squash, corn, green beans, and chili strips along with the cooked broth to make a fairly wet stew.

Cook slowly until the vegetables are done, about 15 or 20 minutes. Taste the stew and adjust the seasoning. Stir in the cheese and chopped cilantro.

Serve with cornbread or tortillas, and garnish with whole leaves of cilantro.

A great one-dish meal if you have a garden or have just visited the Farmer's Market.

TORTILLA SOUP

★

Representative Tom Udall, NEW MEXICO

1   tablespoon onion, finely chopped
1   clove garlic, minced
2   tablespoons shortening
2   cups soup stock or 2 bouillon cubes dissolved in
    2 cups water
¼   teaspoon ground cumin
    Salt to taste
3   dried red chili pods, cleaned and cut in strips
1   cup grated longhorn, cheddar, or Swiss cheese
    Corn chips

In deep saucepan, saute onion and garlic in shortening. Add stock, cumin, and salt. Add strips of chili and boil slowly until chili is tender.

Before serving, add grated cheese. Stir. Serve on half bowl of corn chips.

Serves 4.

A soup to complement any meal.

BASQUE VEGETABLE SOUP

Representative Bill Thomas, CALIFORNIA

4   carrots, sliced
4   celery stalks, sliced
6   potatoes, cubed
1   onion, diced
6   cloves of garlic, minced
1   head of cabbage, chopped
4   teaspoons chicken bouillon granules
1   15-ounce can tomato sauce
3   quarts water

Combine all ingredients and simmer for 3 hours. Serve with pinto beans, salsa, and French bread.

Hearty and healthy.

UNITED STATES HOUSE OF REPRESENTATIVES BEAN SOUP

★

Representative Joe Barton, TEXAS

Representative David E. Bonior, MICHIGAN

2 pounds Number 1 Michigan beans
Smoked ham hock
Salt to taste
Pepper to taste

Cover with cold water and soak overnight.

Drain and cover with water again.

Add a smoked ham hock and simmer slowly for about 4 hours until beans are cooked and tender. Salt and pepper to suit taste. Just before serving, bruise beans with large spoon or ladle, enough to cloud.

Makes 6 servings.

Bean soup has been a featured item on the menu of the House of Representatives Restaurant since long before that day in 1904 when the Speaker of the House, Joseph G. Cannon, of Illinois, came into the House Restaurant and ordered bean soup.

Then, as now, bean soup was a hearty, zesty, and filling dish; but on that particular day in Washington, it was hot and humid, and bean soup had therefore been omitted from the menu. "Thunderation," roared Speaker Cannon, "I had my mouth set for bean soup." He continued, "From now on, hot or cold, rain, snow or shine, I want it on the menu every day."

And so it has been—bean soup on the menu every single day since.

LENTIL BARLEY STEW

Representative Michael Castle, DELAWARE

½ cup butter
⅓ cup onion, chopped
½ cup celery, chopped
1 pound stewed tomatoes
2 cups water
½ cup lentils, well rinsed
⅓ cup medium barley
½ teaspoon salt
   Dash of pepper
¼ teaspoon crushed rosemary
⅓ cup carrots, shredded
1 teaspoon sugar (optional)
   Crushed red pepper (optional)

Melt butter in large heavy saucepan over moderate heat. Add onion and celery and cook until onion is lightly browned. Stir in tomatoes, water, lentils, barley, salt, pepper, and rosemary. Bring to a boil. Cover tightly and boil gently for 25 minutes, stirring occasionally.

Add carrots and cook 5 minutes longer.

May be frozen.

Makes 6 servings.

Please note: I add a teaspoon of sugar to reduce the acidity of the tomatoes. Also for a little zip, add a few shakes of crushed red pepper.

KAY'S SHADYWOOD
SHOWDOWN CHILI

★

Senator Kay Bailey Hutchinson, TEXAS

2 medium yellow onions, diced

2 green peppers, diced

1 tablespoon olive oil

2½ pounds ground sirloin

¼ cup mole sauce

1 16-ounce can tomato sauce

4 cups water

¼ cup chili powder

Salt to taste

Pepper to taste

Garlic powder to taste

1 16-ounce can kidney beans (optional)

Saute half of the onions and peppers in 1 tablespoon olive oil. Brown meat separately, leaving chunks. Drain fat. Add onion and pepper mixture to meat. Add 3 tablespoons mole sauce to mixture.

Transfer to large pot. Add tomato sauce, water, and 3 tablespoons chili powder. Bring to boil. Add remaining mole, if desired, and salt, pepper, and garlic powder to taste. Simmer 1 hour, stirring occasionally.

Saute remaining onions and peppers. Add to pot, along with drained beans. Add final chili powder to taste.

Finish heating and serve with favorite fixin's.

CAPE COD FISH CHOWDER

Senator Edward Kennedy, MASSACHUSETTS

- 2 pounds fresh haddock
- 2 ounces salt pork, diced (or 2 tablespoons butter or margarine)
- 2 medium onions, sliced
- 1 cup celery, chopped
- 4 large potatoes, diced
- 1 bay leaf, crumbled
- 1 quart milk
- 2 tablespoons butter or margarine
- 1 teaspoon salt
  Freshly ground pepper to taste

Simmer haddock in 2 cups of water for 15 minutes. Drain off and reserve broth. Remove skin and bones from fish.

Saute diced salt pork in a large pot until crisp. Remove cooked salt pork. Saute onions in pork fat or butter until golden brown. Add fish, celery, potatoes, and bay leaf.

Measure reserved fish broth plus enough boiling water to make 3 cups liquid. Add to pot and simmer for 30 minutes. Add milk and butter and simmer for an additional 5 minutes or until well heated. Add salt and pepper to taste.

Makes 8 servings.

Even if you have never walked the beach at Cape Cod, the thought conjures up fleets of fishing boats and this favorite food of the Cape. Enjoy this hearty New England favorite of mine!

BACON AND BEAN CHOWDER

★

Senator Chuck Grassley, IOWA

    1   cup navy or pea beans, drained
    1   quart water
    6   slices bacon, diced
    1   onion, chopped
    2   teaspoons pepper
 1⅓   cups potato, diced
 1⅓   cups celery, including leaves, diced
 1½   cups carrots, sliced
    1   29-ounce can tomatoes
    2   tablespoons flour
    2   cups hot milk
        Dried parsley
        American cheese, grated

Combine beans and water in a large kettle. Bring to a boil and cook for 2 minutes. Remove from heat and let stand for 1 hour. Cook bacon and onion until lightly browned. Add, with fat, to beans.

Bring to a boil again. Cover and simmer for 1 hour. Add potato, celery, carrots, and tomatoes. Simmer 30 minutes longer.

Blend flour with a little cold water and stir into soup. Cook until slightly thickened. Add hot milk and additional seasoning, if necessary. Stir in dried parsley and cheese.

Makes about 2 quarts.

> Florence is one of the best cooks I know, and I'm sure that she won't mind sharing her recipe with you.

SEAFOOD GUMBO

Senator John Breaux, LOUISIANA

- 1 cup flour
- 1 cup cooking oil
- 2½ quarts hot water
- 2 cups onion, chopped
- ½ cup green onion tops chopped
- ¼ cup parsley, chopped
- 1 tablespoon salt
- 1 teaspoon cayenne or red pepper
- 1 pound crabmeat or 2 cans crabmeat
- 2 pounds shrimp, raw and peeled
- 1 pint oysters with liquid

To make roux, mix flour and oil together in a 4-cup measure. Microwave on high for 7 minutes. Stir well. Microwave on high for 30 seconds. Stir again and cook 30 seconds more.

To make gumbo, add roux, hot water, onion, green onion tops, parsley, salt, and pepper to a large cooking pot.

Cover and cook on high for 15 minutes. Add crabmeat, shrimp, and oysters and cook on medium for 20 minutes.

Serve as a soup with rice.

CURRIED PEA SOUP

Senator Christopher Bond, MISSOURI

1   10-ounce package frozen peas
1   medium onion, sliced
1   small carrot, sliced
1   rib of celery with leaves, sliced
1   medium potato, sliced
1   garlic clove, crushed
1   teaspoon salt
1   teaspoon curry powder
2   cups chicken stock, divided
1   cup heavy cream

Place vegetables, seasonings, and 1 cup of stock in a saucepan and bring to a boil. Cover, reduce heat, and simmer 20 to 30 minutes until vegetables are very tender. Transfer vegetables to a food processor or blender. Puree. With the motor running, pour in remaining stock and the cream. Chill. Garnish each portion with whipped cream and a mint leaf.

To serve hot, omit adding cream in food processor or blender. Instead, process puree and stock only. Heat. Remove from heat and stir in cream. Garnish with a teaspoon of sour cream and crisply cooked, crumbled bacon.

Makes 4 to 6 servings.

WATERCRESS SOUP

Senator Christopher Bond, MISSOURI

6 cups watercress
3 tablespoons butter, divided
¼ cup onion, minced
1½ cups water
1 teaspoon salt
½ teaspoon white pepper
½ teaspoon curry powder
2 tablespoons flour
2 14½-ounce cans chicken broth
2 cups milk
2 egg yolks
1 cup heavy cream

Rinse and drain watercress. Remove coarsest stems. Reserve. Melt 1 tablespoon butter in a large saucepan. Add onion and cook until golden. Add watercress, water, salt, pepper, and curry powder. Cook over high heat for 5 minutes.

Transfer mixture to a food processor or blender. Puree. Melt remaining 2 tablespoons butter in a saucepan and stir in flour. Add chicken broth and milk; bring to a boil. Stir in watercress mixture.

Combine egg yolks and heavy cream and beat until slightly thickened. Stir 1 cup of hot soup into egg and cream mixture. Add to remaining soup, stirring constantly. Heat, but do not boil. Garnish with croutons and a sprig of watercress.

Makes 8 servings.

> While I fish for trout from the back of the canoe, my wife usually is at the bow searching for watercress. A fall float trip on the Eleven Point River yielded a bumper crop and led to the development of this refreshing soup. We enjoy it as a prelude to a light luncheon or patio supper.

SAUSAGE ZUCCHINI SOUP

Senator Christopher Bond, MISSOURI

1¼ pounds mild Italian sausage without casings
1½ cups celery, sliced
4 pounds fresh tomatoes, peeled and cut in wedges
1½ cups tomato juice
1 teaspoon salt
1½ teaspoons Italian seasoning (or a mixture of basil and oregano)
1 teaspoon sugar
¼ teaspoon garlic salt
2 green peppers, cut into 1-inch pieces
1½ pounds zucchini, cut into ½-inch slices
1 cup mozzarella cheese, shredded

Crumble sausage into a 4-quart saucepan; brown and drain fat. Add celery and cook 10 minutes. Add tomatoes, juice, and seasonings and simmer for 10 minutes. Stir in green peppers. Cook for 5 minutes.

Add zucchini and cook 1 to 2 minutes, until barely heated. Caution: Do not overcook zucchini. Sprinkle mozzarella cheese over the top.

Serve immediately.

Note: If more liquid is desired, add more tomato juice. Two 28-ounce cans Italian plum tomatoes may be substituted for fresh tomatoes.

Makes 8 to 10 servings.

During a visit to Rolla for the annual St. Patrick's Day festivities, we sampled this substantial and satisfying soup at the home of a friend. Ladle into sizable soup bowls and serve in front of a crackling fire.

MISSOURI APPLE SOUP

★

Senator Christopher Bond, MISSOURI

2 tablespoons butter

2 medium onions, thinly sliced

6 red Jonathan apples, peeled, cored, and diced

4 cups chicken broth

2 tablespoons sugar

1 tablespoon curry powder

Salt to taste

Freshly ground white pepper to taste

1 to 2 cups light cream

In a Dutch oven, melt butter and saute onions until transparent. Add apples, broth, sugar, and curry powder. Season with salt and pepper. Cook covered over low heat until apples are soft. Strain apples and onions from broth and reserve. Set broth aside.

Place apples and onions in a food processor or blender. Puree. Add broth and blend well. Add cream according to desired richness. Chill. Taste and adjust seasoning. Garnish with thin apple wedges and a sprinkling of sliced almonds.

Makes 10 to 12 servings.

Stephenson's Apple Orchard in eastern Jackson County is a name that brings to mind family outings during the fall picking season and bushel baskets heaping with succulent apples.

POLISH SAUSAGE STEW

Senator Chuck Grassley, IOWA

1   10½-ounce can cream of celery soup
⅓   cup light brown sugar
1   16-ounce can sauerkraut, drained
2   pounds Polish sausage, cut in chunks
4   medium potatoes, cubed
1   cup onion, chopped
1   cup Monterey Jack cheese, shredded

Combine in a Crock-Pot the soup, sugar, and sauerkraut. Add the sausage, potatoes, and onion. Cook on low for 8 hours or on high for 4 hours. Skim off fat and stir in cheese just before serving.

Makes 4 to 6 servings.

Jolene, our friend, brought this to our house for supper one night.

CHARLESTON SHE-CRAB SOUP

Senator Ernest Hollings, SOUTH CAROLINA

2 tablespoons butter

2 teaspoons flour

2 cups whole milk

½ cup cream

½ teaspoon ground mace

¼ teaspoon celery salt

1 tablespoon Worcestershire sauce

1 pound lump crabmeat (with roe if possible)

Salt to taste

Pepper to taste

TO SERVE:

Sherry (warmed in a pitcher)

Melt butter in top of double boiler and blend in flour until smooth. Add milk, very slowly, stirring. Add cream. To this add mace, celery salt, and Worcestershire sauce. Add crabmeat and fold gently. Heat to piping hot. Add salt and pepper. Pass sherry at table; diners can add it to taste.

Makes 4 to 6 servings.

Charleston, South Carolina, our hometown, is a port city and being such abounds in seafood cookery. She-crab soup is a particular favorite of ours, and we hope you enjoy it!

SANTA FE CUCUMBER SOUP

Senator Pete Domenici, NEW MEXICO

3   medium cucumbers, peeled and chunked
1   clove garlic
3   cups chicken broth (canned, from cubes, or homemade)
3   cups commercial sour cream
1   tablespoon vinegar
2   teaspoons salt

ASSORTED GARNISHES:
Chopped parsley
Fresh tomatoes, chopped
Bacon bits
Croutons
Thinly sliced green onions, including tops
Chopped green peppers
Chopped salted cashews or almonds

Combine cucumbers and garlic in blender. Add a little chicken broth. Whirl until smooth, then blend in remaining broth. Stir in sour cream. Add vinegar and salt. Cover and chill thoroughly.

Serve in small bowls. Pass around garnishes, each in a different bowl or cup; serve as many or as few as you wish.

Delicious and fun. Garnishes for all tastes.

OYSTER STEW

Representative Howard Coble, NORTH CAROLINA

2   quarts whole milk
1   pint shucked select oysters
2   tablespoons butter
    Salt to taste
    Pepper to taste

Combine all ingredients. Cook over low heat. Heat to simmering, but do not boil. Serve piping hot with crackers.

Note: For a slightly thicker stew, stir 1 or 2 tablespoons flour into a small amount of milk until smooth. Add to pot and heat to piping hot.

This dish is particularly tasty during the winter months and is particularly easy for us bachelors to prepare.

BRAZOS RIVER STEW

Representative Tom DeLay, TEXAS

3   slices bacon

1   pound stew beef cubes

1   16-ounce can tomatoes

2   cups beef broth or bouillon

1   cup water

2   stalks celery, sliced

2   medium onions, chopped

2   garlic cloves, minced

2   tablespoons Worcestershire sauce

1   teaspoon chili powder

1   tablespoon flour

    Salt to taste

    Pepper to taste

4   medium carrots, coarsely sliced

4   small potatoes, peeled

1   8-ounce can kernel corn

Fry bacon in a Dutch oven or large stew pot. Remove bacon strips and drain on paper towel; leave fat in pot. Add stew meat to pot and sear. Lower heat and add tomatoes, beef broth, water, celery, onion, garlic, Worcestershire sauce, and chili powder. Cover and simmer 2 hours.

Remove ¼ cup broth from stew; cool and mix with flour. Add flour mixture to stew. Add salt and pepper as needed. Add carrots and potatoes and cook 30 minutes. Add corn and crumbled bacon strips; cook another 5 minutes. Serve in large bowls.

Makes 5 or 6 servings.

TOMATO BASIL SOUP

Representative Jim Turner, TEXAS

½ cup onion, chopped
½ cup green pepper, chopped
1   tablespoon margarine
½ teaspoon dried basil
2   cups tomato juice
1   cup buttermilk

In medium saucepan, saute onion and green pepper in margarine until tender; stir in remaining ingredients.

Transfer to blender, in several batches, and puree until smooth. Return to saucepan and heat until warm; do not let boil.

Makes 4 servings.

Just like La Madeleine's restaurant . . . but a healthier version.

NEW ENGLAND CLAM CHOWDER

★

Representative Paul Kanjorski, PENNSYLVANIA

¼	pound salt bacon
1	large Spanish onion, chopped
3	bottles Doxsee clam juice (6 to 8 ounces each)
4	large potatoes, peeled and sliced
21	ounces whole baby clams
1½	quarts half-and-half

Finely chop bacon and begin browning. Add onion and brown until clear. Add clam juice, potatoes, and clams to mixture and heat until potatoes are tender.

Add half-and-half and heat until close to boiling. If necessary, add regular milk to dilute to desired consistency. Serve immediately with oyster crackers.

Note: Do not add half-and-half until ready to serve. Before adding milk, the mixture may even be refrigerated until serving time.

Makes 12 servings.

VIDALIA ONION SOUP

Senator Zell Miller, GEORGIA

2 Vidalia onions, finely chopped

¼ cup butter

½ cup flour

1 14½-ounce can chicken broth

3 cups milk

⅓ cup white wine

½ teaspoon thyme

2 bay leaves

½ teaspoon salt

1 teaspoon garlic powder

½ cup peanuts, finely chopped

Saute onions in butter until tender. Mix flour and chicken broth and add to onion mixture. Add milk, wine, and spices. Simmer slowly for 20 minutes. Remove bay leaves. Before serving, garnish with chopped peanuts.

Serves 6.

When Senator Miller was governor of Georgia, he always tried to serve Georgia-grown food at the Governor's Mansion. This Vidalia soup recipe was one of the most requested dishes that was served at functions held at the mansion.

And, you can only grow these onions in a certain area in south Georgia. Each year since coming to Washington, D.C., he has provided each senator with a 10-pound bag of Vidalias dug right out of the fields of south Georgia.

CAULIFLOWER SOUP

Senator Joseph Lieberman, CONNECTICUT

3 tablespoons butter or margarine
3 tablespoons flour
⅛ teaspoon nutmeg
3⅔ cups chicken broth
1 cup water
3 cups small cauliflowerets
1 egg yolk
3 tablespoons heavy cream
Snipped fresh parsley

In a medium saucepan, melt butter or margarine and blend in flour and nutmeg. Slowly stir in broth and water, then bring to a boil while stirring. Add cauliflowerets. Simmer soup, covered, about 25 minutes or until cauliflowerets are tender.

In a small bowl, mix egg yolk with cream, stirring until blended. Add to soup. Bring soup just to boiling point, stirring constantly. Serve in small bowls. Sprinkle with parsley.

Makes 6 servings.

Soup is a favorite beginning to a Czechoslovakian meal. It is usually served with tasty additions like the cauliflower.

VEGETARIAN CHILI

★

Senator Bill Nelson, FLORIDA

2½ cups kidney beans
 1 teaspoon salt
 1 cup tomato juice
 1 cup raw bulgur
 4 cloves garlic, crushed
1½ cups onion, chopped
 3 tablespoons olive oil
 1 cup carrots, chopped
 1 cup celery, chopped
 2 teaspoons ground cumin
 1 teaspoon basil
 1 teaspoon chili powder
   Salt to taste
   Pepper to taste
   Dash of cayenne pepper
 2 cups tomatoes, chopped
 ½ lemon, juiced
 3 tablespoons tomato paste
 3 tablespoons dry red wine
 ¼ cup grated cheddar cheese
 2 teaspoons parsley, chopped

Soak kidney beans in water to cover, 3 to 4 hours. Add more water and salt. Cook until tender, about 1 hour.

Heat tomato juice to a boil. Pour over bulgur. Cover and let stand at least 15 minutes. Saute garlic and onions in olive oil. Add carrots, celery, spices, and seasonings (all except cayenne pepper).

When vegetables are almost cooked, add cayenne pepper. Combine beans and vegetable mixture with tomatoes, lemon juice, tomato paste, and wine. Cover and heat in 350-degree oven. Garnish with cheese and parsley.

Makes 6 to 8 servings.

SENATOR LINCOLN'S WHITE CHILI

★

Senator Blanche Lincoln, ARKANSAS

1	medium onion, chopped
2	garlic cloves, minced
1	tablespoon olive oil
½	cup green chilies, chopped
2	teaspoons ground cumin
1½	teaspoons oregano
¼	teaspoon ground cloves
2¼	teaspoons cayenne pepper
8	cups great northern beans, canned
6	cups chicken broth
6 to 8	boneless chicken breasts
3	cups Monterey Jack cheese, grated
	Sour cream
	Salsa

Saute onions and garlic in oil in a large skillet. Add green chilies and seasonings. Add undrained beans and chicken broth. Chop chicken breasts into cubes. Add chicken to skillet mixture and cook for 20 to 30 minutes. Add 1 cup of Monterey Jack cheese and stir until melted.

Serve in bowls with remaining grated Monterey Jack cheese, salsa, and sour cream as toppings.

FAMOUS SENATE RESTAURANT BEAN SOUP

Senator Jack Reed, RHODE ISLAND

2 pounds small navy beans

4 quarts water

1½ pounds ham hocks

1 onion, chopped

2 tablespoons butter

Salt to taste

Pepper to taste

Wash navy beans and run through hot water until beans are white again. Place beans in a large pot with water and ham hocks. Boil slowly for 3 hours, covered.

Braise the onion in butter until light brown. Add to bean soup. Season with salt and pepper, then serve. Do not add salt until ready to serve.

Serves 8.

Whatever uncertainties may exist in the Senate of the United States, one thing is sure: Bean soup is on the menu of the Senate Restaurant every day.

The origin of the culinary decree has been lost in antiquity, but there are several oft-repeated legends.

One story has it that Senator Fred Thomas Dubois of Idaho, who served in the Senate from 1901 to 1907 and was chairman of the committee that supervised the Senate Restaurant, gaveled through a resolution requiring that bean soup be on the menu every day.

Another account attributes the bean soup mandate to Senator Knute Nelson of Minnesota, who expressed his fondness for it in 1903.

In any case, senators and their guests are always assured of a hearty, nourishing dish. They know they can rely on its delightful flavor and epicurean qualities.

SANTA FE SOUP

Representative Spencer Bachus, ALABAMA

2   pounds turkey or beef, chopped
1   onion, chopped
1   package ranch-style dressing mix
2   packages taco seasoning mix
1   16-ounce can black beans, undrained
1   16-ounce can kidney beans, undrained
1   16-ounce can pinto beans, undrained
1   16-ounce can diced tomatoes with chilies, undrained
1   16-ounce can tomato wedges, undrained
2   16-ounce cans white corn, undrained
2   cups water
    Sour cream
    Cheddar cheese, shredded
    Green onions, chopped

Cook meat and onion together until meat is browned. Stir ranch-style dressing mix and taco seasoning mix into meat. Add remaining ingredients with juices from all. Add water. Simmer for 2 hours. If mixture is too thick, add additional water.

Garnish each serving with sour cream, shredded cheese, and green onions.

Serve with tortilla chips.

Makes 4 quarts.

SIDE DISHES

★ 4

Vegetables,
Potatoes,
Grains,
and Beans

BROCCOLI CASSEROLE

Representative Thomas Carper, DELAWARE

¼ cup onion, finely chopped

6 tablespoons margarine, divided

2 tablespoons flour

½ cup water

8 ounces Cheez Whiz

2 packages broccoli, chopped, thawed, and drained

3 eggs, well beaten

½ cup bread crumbs

In a large skillet, saute onions in 4 tablespoons margarine. Add flour and water; cook on low heat until thick. Add Cheez Whiz and combine sauce and broccoli. Add eggs and mix gently until blended.

Place mixture in a greased 1½-quart dish, cover with crumbs, and dot with rest of margarine. Bake at 325 degrees for 30 minutes.

Makes 8 servings.

ZUCCHINI AND CHERRY TOMATOES

★

Senator Christopher Bond, MISSOURI

5 small zucchini
¼ cup butter
¼ cup onion, finely chopped
½ clove garlic, minced
¾ cup cherry tomatoes, halved
  Salt to taste
  Freshly ground pepper to taste
2 tablespoons sesame seeds, toasted
¼ cup parsley, finely chopped

Slice zucchini on the bias into ½-inch slices. In a 4-quart pan of rapidly boiling water, blanch zucchini for 1 minute. Rinse with cold water, drain, and pat dry.

Melt butter, add onion and garlic, and saute until soft and golden brown. Add zucchini, cover, and cook for 2 minutes. Add tomatoes, cover, and cook for 1 minute. Season with salt and pepper. Add sesame seed and parsley. Toss. Adjust seasonings to taste.

Makes 6 servings.

A trip to the state fair in Sedalia is an annual family ritual. Our son Sam loves the excitement of the midway, the children's barnyard, and the many agricultural and livestock displays. The giant zucchini are amazing, but the homegrown ones are fine in this tasty vegetable duo.

BEETS IN SOUR CREAM SAUCE

★

Senator Philip Crane, ILLINOIS

¼ cup sour cream
1 tablespoon vinegar
1 teaspoon green onions, chopped
¾ teaspoon sugar
½ teaspoon salt
  Dash of cayenne pepper
2½ cups beets, cooked and drained

Combine first 6 ingredients in a saucepan. Add drained beets. Heat slowly and stir to coat each beet evenly. Do not boil. Makes 6 to 8 servings.

COLESLAW

Senator Christopher Bond, MISSOURI

12 ounces sour cream

2 tablespoons mayonnaise

3 tablespoons vinegar

4 tablespoons sugar

¼ teaspoon garlic salt

½ teaspoon salt

Pepper to taste

1 large head cabbage

5 carrots, sliced

1 red pepper, seeded

1 green pepper, seeded

1 bunch green onions

Combine sour cream, mayonnaise, vinegar, sugar, garlic salt, salt, and pepper for dressing. Quarter cabbage and slice thinly. Do not cut too finely.

Peel carrots and slice very thinly into rounds. Chop peppers and onions. Pour dressing mixture over cabbage, carrots, peppers, and onions. Toss and refrigerate.

Makes 12 servings.

When Sam and I are lucky enough to find the white bass running at the Lake of the Ozarks, our fish fry includes this tangy coleslaw, plus corn on the cob and sauteed zucchini.

SOUFFLÉED CORN

Senator Christopher Bond, MISSOURI

6 ears corn
¾ cup butter, divided
½ cup sugar, divided
1 tablespoon flour
1½ teaspoons baking powder
½ cup evaporated milk
2 eggs, well beaten
1 teaspoon cinnamon

Preheat oven to 350 degrees. Cut corn kernels from cob. Melt ½ cup butter. Stir in ¼ cup sugar. Gradually add flour and baking powder. Blend in milk and eggs, then add corn. Mix well. Pour into a greased 8-inch round baking dish. Bake 35 minutes or until done. Remove from oven.

Melt remaining butter and combine with remaining sugar and the cinnamon. Brush on top of soufflé while soufflé is still hot.

Makes 6 to 8 servings.

Freshly picked corn is one of the treats of summer in Missouri.

LEMON YAM PUFF

Senator Christopher Bond, MISSOURI

4 pounds yams
1 cup brown sugar, packed
½ cup butter, softened
½ teaspoon salt
2 teaspoons orange rind, grated
2 teaspoons lemon rind, grated

Preheat oven to 350 degrees. Cook unpeeled whole sweet potatoes in boiling water for 30 minutes or until tender. Drain and reserve liquid.

Peel potatoes and mash until smooth. If mixture seems dry, add some reserved liquid. Add remaining ingredients and beat until light and fluffy.

Transfer to a greased 2-quart casserole. Bake for 30 minutes and serve hot.

Makes 8 to 10 servings.

This wintertime favorite has its origins in Sainte Genevieve County. French settlers founded the community prior to 1750. My ancestors were among the earliest to take up residence on the Missouri side of the Mississippi River. One member of the family was a member of the convention that framed the Missouri Constitution.

HEARTY
RICE CASSEROLE

★

Representative Jim Turner, TEXAS

1¼ cups Monterey Jack cheese, grated
1 cup part-skim ricotta cheese
1 cup mayonnaise (may use low-fat)
1 clove garlic, peeled and crushed
¼ teaspoon pepper
3 cups white rice, cooked
1 10-ounce package frozen broccoli, thawed and chopped
1 cup green peas, thawed
¼ cup green onions, thinly sliced

Mix all ingredients, reserving ¼ cup of the Monterey Jack cheese for topping. Bake uncovered in 2-quart baking dish sprayed with cooking spray at 350 degrees for 25 minutes, putting remaining cheese on top for last 5 minutes of baking.

Serves 8.

An attractive dish . . . and a good one!

BAKED SPINACH

Representative Jim Turner, TEXAS

2 10-ounce packages frozen spinach, chopped
2 cups small-curd cottage cheese (may use low-fat)
1 cup cheddar cheese, grated
2 eggs, beaten
   Salt to taste
   Pepper to taste

Thaw spinach and squeeze dry. Mix with remaining ingredients and place in a greased 9-inch baking dish. Bake at 350 degrees for 40 to 45 minutes or until firm in center.

Serves 6 to 8.

Great way to eat your spinach.

RICE AND MUSHROOM CASSEROLE

Senator Christopher Bond, MISSOURI

2 cups onion, chopped

2 cups fresh mushrooms, sliced

½ cup butter

1 cup beef consommé

1 cup water

1 cup uncooked rice

Salt to taste

Freshly ground pepper to taste

Preheat oven to 350 degrees. Saute onions and mushrooms in butter. Add consommé and water. Mix in rice and season with salt and pepper.

Transfer to a buttered 2-quart casserole. Bake covered for 45 minutes or until done. Garnish with snipped chives.

Makes 6 servings.

My mother is a marvelous cook and introduced my wife to this dish after we were married. It is great with chicken, game, or pork.

NEW POTATOES IN BURNED BUTTER

★

Senator Mike Crapo, IDAHO

10   new potatoes, 1 to 2 inches in diameter
½   cup butter
    Salt to taste
    Pepper to taste

Peel potatoes. Place whole potatoes in saucepan and barely cover with water. Simmer until barely tender. Melt butter in a separate pan; brown until almost ready to burn (this is very tricky).

Place drained new potatoes in a small bowl; drizzle hot butter over potatoes. Cut new potatoes into smaller pieces; season to taste with salt and pepper.

Serves 4.

HASH BROWN CASEROLE

★

Representative Tom Latham, IOWA

2 pounds frozen hash browns
½ cup margarine
1 medium onion, diced
1 10½-ounce can cream of chicken soup
1 small carton whipping cream
1 8-ounce tub sour cream
2 cups cheddar cheese, shredded
2 cups Rice Krispies

Place frozen hash browns in a 9- by 13-inch glass dish. Melt ¼ cup margarine, add diced onion, and saute until tender. Remove from heat and let cool 5 minutes.

Add soup, whipping cream, sour cream, and shredded cheese to margarine and onions. Mix well and pour over top of hash browns.

Melt remaining ¼ cup of margarine, add Rice Krispies, and pour on top of hash browns.

Bake uncovered at 350 degrees for 1 hour.

(May be prepared ahead of time and refrigerated overnight.)

TOMATOES
FLORENTINE

★ ─────────────────────────────────

Representative Jim Turner, TEXAS

6   large ripe tomatoes
2   tablespoons olive oil
¾   cup onion, finely chopped
½   cup Italian bread crumbs
½   teaspoon salt
¼   teaspoon pepper
1   10-ounce package frozen chopped spinach,
     thawed and squeezed dry
2   tablespoons Parmesan cheese, grated

Cut a ½-inch slice from the top of each tomato. Carefully scoop out pulp (a melon baller works well). Chop the pulp. Drain and set aside. Place tomato shells upside down on paper towels to drain.

In a large skillet, heat olive oil; add onion and saute for 2 minutes. Stir in bread crumbs, salt, pepper, chopped tomato, and spinach; cook and stir until hot.

Spoon mixture into tomatoes. Top with Parmesan cheese. Place in a lightly greased 8- by 8-inch baking dish and bake uncovered at 350 degrees for about 30 minutes.

Makes 6 servings.

Pretty on a plate!

BLACK BEAN
SALAD

Representative Jim Turner, TEXAS

2 pounds fresh parsley, chopped

2 tablespoons lime juice

½ teaspoon salt

½ teaspoon pepper

2 15-ounce cans black beans, rinsed and drained

1 cup fresh tomato, chopped

1 avocado, diced

4 tablespoons green onions, chopped

2 tablespoons jalapeno, chopped and seeded

Combine first 4 ingredients in large bowl. Stir well with a whisk. Add remaining ingredients, tossing well. Cover and chill 2 hours. Serve over salad greens.

Makes 6 to 8 servings.

> Easy healthy and delicious. . . . Only 112 calories and 2.1 grams of fat per serving.

EGGPLANT DELUXE

Representative Jim Turner, TEXAS

1   6-ounce package Stove Top stuffing, chicken flavor
1   large eggplant, peeled and cubed
1   10½-ounce can cream of celery soup
1   egg, slightly beaten
½   cup cheddar cheese, grated, divided

Prepare stuffing mix according to box directions; set aside. Drop eggplant cubes into small amount of boiling water. Cook, covered, until tender, about 5 to 10 minutes; drain and mash slightly. Combine eggplant, stuffing, celery soup, egg, and ¼ cup of cheese. Place in greased 1½-quart casserole and top with remaining cheese. Bake at 350 degrees until cheese is bubbly and casserole is brown around the edges, around 40 minutes.

This tastes so good, you may not recognize it as eggplant.

ONE-STEP SWEET POTATOES

Representative Jim Turner, TEXAS

1   40-ounce can sweet potatoes, drained
¼   cup margarine, cut into pieces
1   8-ounce can crushed pineapple, drained
½   cup pure maple syrup
    Miniature marshmallows for topping

Place all ingredients, except marshmallows, into a greased 1½-quart baking dish. Combine ingredients, using a potato masher, until well mixed. Bake at 350 degrees until bubbly, about 40 minutes.

Top with marshmallows, and continue baking 10 minutes or until marshmallows are lightly browned.

Makes 6 servings.

> No mixing bowls to clean up!

GRANDMA DAIGLE'S RICE DRESSING

★

Senator John Breaux, LOUISIANA

1   pound ground beef
3   tablespoons cooking oil
½   cup green onion, chopped
1   cup celery, chopped
1   large green pepper, chopped
1   cup water
3   cups cooked rice
½   cup parsley, chopped
   Salt to taste
   Pepper to taste
2   tablespoons Kitchen Bouquet (optional)

Cook meat in oil in a large pot until brown. Add onions, celery, and green pepper. Reduce heat and cook until wilted. Add water (add more water if needed to keep about the same amount of juice that you started with). Add seasonings. Add to cooked rice and keep warm until ready to serve.

Serves 10 to 12.

SOUTHERN SWEET
POTATO RING

★

Senator John Breaux, LOUISIANA

8   medium sweet potatoes or 1 large can
9   tablespoons butter, softened
½   cup light brown sugar
1   5-ounce can evaporated milk
1   teaspoon nutmeg
1   teaspoon cinnamon
1   teaspoon vanilla
1   egg
½   cup dark brown sugar
1½   cups pecan halves

Bake sweet potatoes and remove peel. In a large bowl, mash potatoes with a fork or put in food processor. Add butter, light brown sugar, milk, nutmeg, cinnamon, vanilla, and egg. Mix well.

Generously grease a Bundt pan with cooking spray or butter. Sprinkle dark brown sugar in bottom of pan, followed by pecan halves, then spoon in the sweet potato mixture.

Bake at 350 degrees for 1 hour. Let cool 15 minutes before removing from the mold.

Makes 8 to10 servings.

Great for the holidays!

SUMMER SQUASH CASSEROLE

Representative Steve Buyer, INDIANA

9 small yellow squash
4 eggs
1 cup sugar
¾ cup butter or margarine
⅓ medium onion, chopped
Salt to taste
Pepper to taste

Clean and cut squash into small cubes. Boil until tender. Drain and mash with potato masher. Add remaining ingredients.

Place in an 8- by 8-inch casserole coated with nonstick spray. Bake uncovered for 1½ hours at 350 degrees. Remove when golden brown.

Serve hot with crusty bread!

ARIZONA BAKED BEANS

Senator John McCain, ARIZONA

1   medium onion, chopped
1   teaspoon butter
1   16-ounce can red kidney beans
1   16-ounce can B&M baked beans
1   cup ketchup
1   cup brown sugar, packed
1   tablespoon vinegar
1   teaspoon mustard
4   strips fried bacon, cooled and crumbled

In a skillet, saute chopped onion in butter. In a large baking pot combine kidney beans, baked beans, ketchup, brown sugar, vinegar, mustard, and bacon.

After combining and stirring enough to mix the ingredients, add the sauteed onion. Mix well. Bake in a covered dish at 350 degrees for 35 minutes or until piping hot.

Makes 10 servings.

A wonderful Southwest taste treat!

MARINATED BROCCOLI

Representative David L. Hobson, OHIO

3 stalks broccoli
1 cup vinegar
½ cup oil
1 tablespoon sugar
1 tablespoon dill weed
1 teaspoon garlic salt
1 teaspoon salt
1 teaspoon pepper

Wash broccoli and break into flowerets. Mix all other ingredients and place in a plastic bag with broccoli.
Refrigerate for 12 hours. To serve, drain the broccoli well.

SCALLOPED EGGPLANT

Representative Ralph Regula, OHIO

1 medium eggplant, peeled and cubed
  Salt to taste
3 tablespoons onion, grated
1 10½-ounce can cream of mushroom soup
1 cup sharp cheese, grated
¾ cup buttered bread crumbs
1 tablespoon butter

Peel and cube eggplant. Cook eggplant until just tender in boiling salted water. Drain well.

Place eggplant in 2-quart baking dish. Sprinkle grated onion over top. Cover with mushroom soup. Sprinkle top with ½ cup grated cheese. Top with buttered bread crumbs. Dot crumbs with butter. Sprinkle remaining cheese over top.

Bake in preheated 350 degree oven for 45 minutes until nicely browned.

Makes 4 servings.

Fantastic side dish, and a great way to enjoy eggplant.

KUGELIS
(POTATO CASSEROLE)

Senator Richard J. Durbin, ILLINOIS

10 large red potatoes
1 large onion
5 strips bacon, diced
½ cup hot milk or evaporated milk
3 eggs
2 teaspoons salt
¼ teaspoon pepper

Peel and grate potatoes. (A food processor makes this job easy.) Grate onion. Fry diced bacon until crisp. Pour bacon fat and bacon over potatoes. Add hot milk. Add eggs one at a time, beating. Add salt and pepper and mix well.

Pour into greased 9- by 13-inch baking pan. Bake in preheated 400-degree oven for 15 minutes. Reduce heat to 375 degrees and bake for 45 minutes or until firm when tested by inserting a knife in center.

Kugelis is an authentic Lithuanian potato side dish. My mother, Ann Durbin, came to this country from Lithuania as a child. Her mother, who was the family's sole support, had to be very frugal with family finances.

My mother feasted on this delicious, yet inexpensive, dish many times while she was growing up in East St. Louis. (East St. Louis is a town in Illinois.) Although this recipe is not her mother's, she tested many kugelis recipes before finding the best one in a very old Lithuanian cookbook.

Anyone who tries this recipe will not be disappointed . . . or hungry!

CORNBREAD STUFFING

★

Representative Bill Archer, TEXAS

1	cup hot chicken broth (or broth from cooked giblets)
8	slices stale bread, broken into pieces (or about 2 cups)
1	cup cornbread, crumbled
½	cup celery, chopped
½	cup onion, chopped
2	tablespoons butter or margarine
½	cup fresh parsley, chopped
2	eggs, beaten
1	cup pecans, chopped
¾	teaspoon salt
¼	teaspoon pepper
1	teaspoon poultry seasoning
4	hard-cooked eggs, chopped

Pour broth over bread crumbs and cornbread and let stand until softened. Saute celery and onions in butter until tender. Combine bread mixture with celery, onions, parsley, raw eggs, chopped pecans, salt, pepper, and poultry seasoning. Mix well and add chopped eggs.

Bake in preheated 350-degree oven in greased casserole for 30 minutes. Or stuff cooled mixture into a turkey.

Note: Oysters sauteed in butter until just cooked through can also be added to dressing.

Makes 8 to 10 servings.

CREAMY WHIPPED POTATOES

★

Representative William Clay, MISSOURI

5 pounds medium potatoes
1 teaspoon salt
1 8-ounce package whipped cream cheese with chives
¼ teaspoon pepper
1 teaspoon garlic powder
6 tablespoon margarine or butter
1 teaspoon salt
1 cup heavy or whipping cream
¼ cup almonds, sliced
   Paprika

About 1½ hours before serving, peel potatoes and cut into quarters. In a 5-quart saucepan over high heat, boil potatoes with 1 teaspoon of salt and enough water to cover. Reduce heat to low; cover and simmer for 20 minutes or until potatoes are tender. Drain well. Preheat oven to 375 degrees. In large bowl, combine potatoes, cream cheese, pepper, garlic powder, 4 tablespoons margarine or butter, and salt.

With potato masher, mash until smooth. Gradually add heavy cream, mixing well after each addition. Grease 9- by 13-inch glass dish. Dot potatoes with 2 tablespoons margarine or butter. Sprinkle with sliced almonds and paprika. Bake for 30 minutes or until top is golden. An hour before serving, put the potatoes in the oven and heat for 30 minutes at 375 degrees.

SAUTEED COLLARD GREENS WITH GARLIC AND SCALLIONS

Representative Charles Rangel, NEW YORK

2 teaspoons olive oil

3 cups collard greens, chopped or shredded

1 clove garlic, minced

2 scallions, minced

1 tablespoon feta cheese, crumbled

In a large nonstick skillet or a wok, heat oil over medium heat. Add collards and garlic and saute, stirring constantly, until collards are just wilted, about 4 or 5 minutes.

Add scallions before the collards are finished cooking. Serve hot, topped with feta cheese.

Optional: Saute a medium-sized chopped ripe tomato with collards and garlic.

MAIN DISHES

★ 5

Casseroles,
Soufflés,
Savory Pies,
and Sandwiches

HAM MOUSSE

Senator Christopher Bond, MISSOURI

4 cups ground cooked ham
1 large onion, diced
½ cup golden raisins
2 to 3 tablespoons dry sherry
1 teaspoon prepared horseradish
½ teaspoon nutmeg
2 teaspoons Dijon mustard
2 tablespoons unflavored gelatin
2 tablespoons cold water
1 cup chicken stock
1 cup heavy cream, whipped
2 tablespoons parsley, finely chopped

Combine ham, onion, and raisins in a food processor. Puree, or put through the finest blade of a meat grinder three times. Combine meat mixture, sherry, horseradish, nutmeg, and mustard. Set aside.

Soften gelatin in cold water for 5 minutes. Bring chicken stock to a boil, add gelatin, and stir over medium heat until dissolved. Add to ham mixture; blanch thoroughly. Cool 10 to 15 minutes. Fold whipped cream and parsley into mixture.

Turn into a well-oiled 5-cup mold. Chill 3 hours or until firm. Unmold on a plate garnished with sweet gherkins or stuffed green olives. Serve with very thin slices of French or rye bread.

Note: Because of its richness, serve the mousse in small portions when using as an entrée.

Makes 16 to 20 servings.

During a July 4th trip to Hannibal for the annual Tom Sawyer Days, we were treated to this deliciously simple ham mousse served with a spicy homemade mustard. The events highlighted are the Tom Sawyer and Becky Thatcher look-alike contest and the fence-painting contest on the banks of the Mississippi River.

CHEESE SOUFFLÉ

★

Senator Chuck Grassley, IOWA

8 slices day-old bread, crusts trimmed

8 slices Old English cheese

2 cups diced ham or cooked chicken (optional)

6 eggs, well beaten

3 cups milk

½ teaspoon salt

½ teaspoon dry mustard

Lay bread in bottom of buttered 9- by 13-inch pan. Top with cheese. Mix eggs, milk, salt, and dry mustard. Pour well-beaten egg mixture over top.

Cover and refrigerate overnight. Before baking, top with crushed cornflakes mixed with melted butter. Note: If you use meat, put it under the cheese.

Bake for 1 hour at 350 degrees. Serve while hot.

Makes 10 servings.

From Nan, whose husband is in the navy.

TAILGATE HERO SANDWICH

Senator Christopher Bond, MISSOURI

1 loaf French bread, crusty
½ cup Italian dressing
½ cup mayonnaise
   Durkee's hot sauce to taste
⅓ pound each smoked turkey, corned beef, ham
⅓ pound each baby Swiss, provolone, New York cheddar
   cheese, thinly sliced
2 medium tomatoes, thinly sliced and drained
2 medium green peppers, thinly sliced into rings
1 red onion, thinly sliced into rings

Cut bread loaf in half lengthwise. Scoop out centers, leaving a ½-inch shell. Spread both halves with Italian dressing. Generously spread mayonnaise over one half and Durkee's sauce over the other.

Layer turkey, corned beef, and ham on both halves together. Layer cheeses on meat, and tomatoes, green peppers, and onion on cheeses. Carefully put halves together. Wrap sandwich tightly with foil and refrigerate. To serve, cut in 2-inch slices. The sandwich may be prepared and refrigerated for up to 48 hours before serving.

Makes 12 to 16 servings.

> Mizzou football has always been a family affair for the Bonds. This colossal sandwich that serves a crowd is our standby for Tiger tailgates. Kit's dad, Art Bond, who rarely missed a home game, was captain of the 1924 team that won the Missouri Valley Championship, defeating Big Ten winner Chicago.

CHICKEN CASSEROLE

Representative Roger Wicker, MISSISSIPPI

2 10-ounce packages frozen broccoli, chopped
1 package Uncle Ben's wild rice mix
6 whole chicken breasts, boiled
1 10½-ounce can cream of mushroom soup
1 10½-ounce can cream of chicken soup
1 cup mayonnaise
¾ teaspoon curry powder
1 tablespoon lemon juice
1 cup sharp cheese, grated

Cook and season broccoli and wild rice according to directions. Cut chicken in large bite-sized pieces. Arrange broccoli around edge with wild rice in center. Put chicken on top.

Mix remaining ingredients (except cheese) together and pour over top. Sprinkle cheese on top.

Bake at 350 degrees for 40 minutes. Freezes well.

This recipe was given to us when we got married. It is great for a Sunday lunch or any time company is coming.

SEAFOOD LASAGNA

Representative Joe Knollenberg, MICHIGAN

3	tablespoons olive oil
1	yellow onion, chopped
4	garlic cloves, minced
5	cups canned plum tomatoes
½	cup white wine
1	tablespoon dry basil
2	teaspoons fennel seeds
	Salt to taste
	Pepper to taste
1	cup cream (milk may be used for less fat)
2	tablespoons pernod (liquor)
2	pounds shrimp, shelled
1	pound scallops (optional)
3	cups ricotta cheese
1	8-ounce package cream cheese
2	eggs
1	small package spinach, cooked and drained
1	pound lump crabmeat
8	lasagna noodles, cooked
1 to 1½	pounds mozzarella

Sauce: Heat olive oil, then add onion and garlic. Saute 5 minutes. Add tomatoes (not all of juice), white wine, basil, fennel, salt, and pepper. Simmer 45 minutes. Add cream (milk optional), pernod, shrimp, and scallops (optional) and simmer 5 minutes. Remove from heat.

Filling: Mix ricotta, cream cheese, and eggs. Beat with wooden spoon. Add spinach and crabmeat.

Layer ingredients starting with the sauce, noodles, filling, and mozzarella. Repeat and end with the mozzarella. Cook at 350 degrees for 50 minutes.

Makes 8 to 10 servings.

May be frozen.

GARLIC ROASTED CHICKEN AND NEW BABY ROSE POTATOES AND SHALLOTS

★

Representative Loretta Sanchez, CALIFORNIA

CHICKEN:

4 whole chicken legs and thighs, unsplit

½ cup extra virgin olive oil

1 tablespoon dried rosemary

1 teaspoon dried thyme

4 to 6 cloves fresh garlic, thinly sliced

Salt to taste

Pepper to taste

NEW BABY ROSE POTATOES AND SHALLOTS:

10 to 12 new baby rose potatoes, quartered

6 to 8 large shallots

3 tablespoons extra virgin olive oil

1 teaspoon caraway seeds

Salt to taste

Pepper to taste

Preheat oven to 450 degrees. Wash chicken and potatoes and towel dry. In a small bowl, mix together olive oil, rosemary, and thyme.

Place unsplit chicken legs into a baking dish and generously brush both sides with the olive oil mixture to marinate. Sprinkle thin slices of garlic over chicken, and salt and pepper to taste.

Cut potatoes into quarters and peel shallots. Combine potatoes and shallots in small baking dish. Add olive oil and stir together to coat thoroughly. Sprinkle caraway seeds over potatoes. Salt and pepper to taste.

Bake chicken and potatoes for 1 hour, occasionally stirring potatoes.

CHICKEN SPECTACULAR

Representative Kevin Brady, TEXAS

1   box Uncle Ben's Original Recipe Long Grain and Wild Rice
1   8-ounce can French-cut green beans
1   pound cooked chicken, chopped
1   onion, chopped
1   10½-ounce can cream of celery soup
1   10½-ounce can cream of mushroom soup
1   cup mayonnaise
1   can water chestnuts, chopped
1   small jar pimentos, optional
2   tablespoons sugar
    Salt to taste
    Pepper to taste

Prepare rice. Combine all ingredients and cook in large casserole dish at 350 degrees for 30 minutes.

My mother has been making this for years and it is one of my all-time favorites, one of those that challenges the depths of self discipline. —Cathy Brady

KING RANCH CHICKEN

Representative Pete Sessions, TEXAS

4 boneless chicken breasts
1 10½-ounce can cream of chicken soup
1 can Rotel diced tomatoes and peppers
2 cups cheddar cheese, shredded, halved
1 bag tortilla chips

Cook chicken breasts—boil, bake, microwave, or BBQ them. Cut the cooked chicken into small squares.

Mix cream of chicken soup and Rotel, including juice. Add 1 cup shredded cheddar cheese. Mix in tortilla chips.

Pour the entire mixture into a 2-quart buttered casserole. Cover with rest of cheese. Cover with plastic wrap and microwave for 6 minutes. If you do not have a microwave, instead cover with foil and bake at 300 degrees for 30 minutes.

SENATOR LANDRIEU'S OVEN JAMBALAYA

Senator Mary Landrieu, LOUISIANA

- 2 cups Uncle Ben's converted rice
- 2 pounds chicken, cut up
- 1 pound sausage, cut up
- 1 cup French onion soup
- 1 cup beef broth
- 8 ounces tomato soup
- ½ cup green onion, chopped
- ½ cup green pepper, chopped
- 4 bay leaves
    Pepper to taste
- 1 teaspoon parsley
- 8 ounces margarine, cut into slices

Mix all ingredients (except margarine) in a baking dish. Place pats of margarine on top. Bake at 350 degrees for 30 minutes.

Simple and satisfying!

TETRAZZINI

★

Representative Sue Myrick, NORTH CAROLINA

1 pound rotini

1 tablespoon margarine or butter

¼ cup Parmesan cheese

4 boneless chicken breasts

2 tablespoons margarine or butter

2 cups chicken broth

⅔ cup flour

4 cups half-and-half

¼ cup sauterne

1 teaspoon salt

¼ cup Parmesan

1 cup mushrooms (optional)

Cook rotini according to directions and drain. Toss with margarine and Parmesan cheese.

Cook chicken, saving broth. Cut chicken into small pieces.

To cook sauce, melt 2 tablespoons of margarine. Mix in chicken broth while adding the flour to thicken. Next add half-and-half. Cook until it thickens and bubbles. Next add the sauterne and salt and let simmer.

Layer noodles, chicken, mushrooms, and sauce in a casserole dish. Cover with ¼ cup Parmesan cheese. Bake at 350 degrees for 25 to 30 minutes.

FRITTATE

Senator Patrick Leahy, VERMONT

¼ cup olive oil

3 medium onions, thinly sliced

1 cup Italian plum tomatoes, drained and coarsely chopped

6 eggs, beaten

¼ cup Parmesan cheese, grated

½ teaspoon salt

Freshly ground pepper to taste

2 tablespoons parsley, chopped

2 tablespoons dried basil

2 tablespoons butter

Heat oil in skillet. Add onions and cook over moderate heat until lightly brown. Add tomatoes and turn up heat. Cook, stirring for 5 minutes. Cool.

Combine eggs with cheese, salt, pepper, parsley, and basil. Add drained onion and tomato mixture. Wipe out skillet with paper towel.

Add butter to skillet and heat to foaming but do not brown. Add egg mixture. Turn heat to very low and cook for 15 minutes or until only bottom is firm.

Place under heated broiler for 30 minutes to set the top. Do not brown. Cut in wedges and serve from pan.

Makes 4 servings.

FAVORITE CHEESE ENCHILADAS

Senator Tim Johnson, SOUTH DAKOTA

½ cup onion, chopped
4 cloves garlic, crushed
3 tablespoons olive oil
2 ounces green chilies, diced
1 pound tomatoes (fresh or canned), cooked, peeled, and chopped
1 cup tomato juice
¼ teaspoon powdered oregano
¼ teaspoon basil
1 cup strong vegetable broth or beef broth
1½ tablespoons cornstarch
¼ cup water
8 corn tortillas

Fantastic flavor!

FILLINGS:

10 ounces sharp cheddar or Monterey Jack cheese
2 or 3 scallions, chopped
¼ cup parsley, chopped
½ cup mushrooms, chopped
¼ cup black olives, sliced

Saute onion and garlic in olive oil until onion is transparent. Add chilies, tomatoes, tomato juice, and herbs. Simmer 5 minutes. Add broth. Dissolve cornstarch in water and stir into sauce. Cook slowly 10 minutes. If sauce is too thick, add a little water.

Place a corn tortilla gently on heated sauce. Remove tortilla when it starts to warm. Arrange some filling ingredients on the saucy side. Roll it up and place in oiled oblong baking dish.

Repeat with remaining tortillas. Pour remaining sauce over rolled-up tortillas. Bake at 350 degrees for 15 to 20 minutes.

Makes 4 servings.

ANN'S CHICKEN POT PIE

Representative Jim Turner, TEXAS

11   ounces Swanson's white meat chicken, drained
15   ounces succotash, drained
 1   10½-ounce can cream of mushroom soup
     Pepper to taste
 1   package frozen deep-dish pie shells (2 shells)

Preheat oven to 375 degrees. In a large bowl, mix chicken, succo-tash, soup, and pepper. Pour into first pie shell.

While second pie shell is still in its tin, trim away only the crimped edge with a knife. Remove the shell from its tin and center it, upright, on top of pie. Let stand a couple of minutes for crusts to soften; crimp edges together. Cut an X into the top of the pie shell to vent.

Put on a cookie sheet and bake at 375 degrees for 5 minutes; reduce heat to 350 degrees and bake about 20 minutes more or until crust is lightly browned.

From Ann Gray, who is the director of Jim's Orange office. She says this is a lifesaver for her. . . . She's always in a hurry and has a hungry teenager at home! She adds a salad in a bag, and the meal is done!

SUNDAY BRUNCH CASSEROLE

★

Senator Jay Rockefeller, WEST VIRGINIA

      4   cups day-old bread, cubed
      2   cups cheddar cheese, grated
     10   eggs, lightly beaten
      4   cups milk
      1   teaspoon dry mustard
      1   teaspoon salt
      ¼   teaspoon onion powder
          Dash of pepper
 8 to 10   strips cooked bacon, crumbled
      ½   cup cooked or canned mushrooms, sliced
      ½   cup tomatoes, peeled and chopped

Place bread in bottom of a greased 2-quart casserole. Sprinkle with cheese. Beat next 6 ingredients together. Pour over cheese and bread.

Sprinkle with bacon, mushrooms, and tomatoes. Refrigerate, covered, up to 24 hours.

Bake, uncovered, in preheated 325-degree oven 1 hour or until set.

Makes 8 servings.

Recipe from Carolanne Griffith, in *Mountain Measures: A Second Serving*, a collection of West Virginia recipes.

GREEN CHILI ENCHILADAS

Representative Tom DeLay, TEXAS

1	large onion, finely chopped
1	tablespoon margarine
12	corn tortillas, cut into quarters
1	10½-ounce can cream of chicken soup
½	cup water
½	cup sour cream
1	4-ounce can green chilies, drained and chopped
2	cups cooked chicken, diced
3	cups cheddar cheese, grated

Lightly saute onion in margarine; set aside. Cover bottom of 2-quart casserole with tortilla pieces.

Stir together soup with water and sour cream. Add green chilies, chicken, and sauteed onion. Cover tortilla pieces with some of chicken mixture, then cover with cheese.

Repeat layering 2 or 3 times, ending with cheese. Bake in preheated 350-degree oven for 30 minutes.

Makes 4 servings.

EASY BUT RICH BEEF CASSEROLE

★

Representative John Dingell, MICHIGAN

1½ pounds stewing beef, trimmed and cut into 2-inch pieces
½ cup red dinner wine
1 10½-ounce can undiluted beef consommé
1 4-ounce can mushrooms, drained
    Salt to taste
    Pepper to taste
1 medium onion, peeled and sliced
¼ cup bread crumbs
¼ cup flour

Combine beef, wine, consommé, mushrooms, salt, pepper, and onion in casserole dish. Mix bread crumbs with flour and stir into mixture.

Cover and bake in preheated 300-degree oven for about 3 hours or until beef is tender.

HOUSTON MEAT AND CHEESE PIE

Representative Tom DeLay, TEXAS

½ pound ground beef
½ cup mayonnaise
½ cup milk
2 eggs
2 tablespoons flour
¾ cup cheddar cheese, grated
⅓ cup green onions, sliced
  Salt to taste
  Pepper to taste
1 9-inch unbaked pastry shell

Brown meat in a medium skillet; drain and set aside.

Blend mayonnaise, milk, eggs, and flour until smooth. Stir in meat, cheese, onion, salt, and pepper. Turn mixture into unbaked pastry shell. Bake at 350 degrees for 35 to 40 minutes.

This freezes well if there is any left over!

Makes 4 to 6 servings.

MIKE'S FAVORITE CHICKEN PIE

★

Representative Mike DeWine, OHIO

- 1   4- to 5-pound chicken
- 1   medium onion
- 1   stalk celery
- 1   single-crust pie pastry
- 6   tablespoons butter or chicken fat
- 6   tablespoons flour
- 2¼ cups chicken broth
- 1   12-ounce can evaporated milk
-     Salt to taste
-     Pepper to taste

Stew chicken with onion and celery in water until tender; cool. Debone chicken and cut into bite-sized pieces (2 to 3 cups meat). Separate fat and broth; reserve.

To prepare crust, roll out 1 recipe of your favorite pastry ¼-inch thick. Cut out shape to fit top of casserole to be used. Prick crust and bake on baking sheet in preheated 375-degree oven until golden.

Meanwhile prepare sauce: Stir together butter and flour in saucepan until well blended and smooth. Gradually add chicken broth and milk, stirring. Season with salt and pepper.

Heat, stirring until slightly thickened. Stir chicken into sauce. Pour into casserole. Bake in preheated 375-degree oven until bubbling. Top with prebaked crust when ready to serve.

My wife can attest to the fact that this recipe is my favorite!

SENATOR'S MIDNIGHT SUPPER

Senator Richard Lugar, INDIANA

2   slices toast

3   eggs

2   tablespoons sour cream or imitation sour cream
    Salt to taste

1   tablespoon butter

1   cup asparagus spears

5   ounces cheddar cheese soup (undiluted)
    Paprika for garnish

Trim crusts from toast. Lightly beat together eggs, sour cream, and salt with a fork. Then melt butter in skillet and scramble egg mixture. In separate pan, heat asparagus spears.

In third pan, heat cheese soup. Place hot, drained asparagus spears on toast. Top with scrambled eggs. Pour cheese soup over top of eggs. Serve with sausage, bacon, or Canadian bacon and a green salad.

Serves 2.

This is the sort of thing Dick likes when he gets home late at night from meetings or speaking engagements. I can put it together in a hurry, and most of the ingredients are always on hand on the pantry shelf. The dish is also good for brunch.
—Char Lugar

EXTRA MEATY LASAGNA

★

Senator Kent Conrad, NORTH DAKOTA

1½ pounds extra-lean ground beef

1 medium onion, chopped

1 pound sweet Italian sausage links

1 16-ounce can seasoned meaty tomato sauce

1 teaspoon oregano

1 teaspoon pepper

1 teaspoon garlic powder

3 quarts water

   Dash of salt

¼ cup vegetable or olive oil

8 ounces lasagna noodles

3 cups low-fat creamed cottage cheese

2 tablespoons dried parsley flakes

1 egg, beaten

1 pound mozzarella cheese, shredded

1 cup grated Parmesan cheese

Brown ground beef and onion. Add a small amount of oil to moisten, if necessary. Remove ground beef and onion. Retain fat in pan and add sausage links. Brown on all sides. In saucepan place tomato sauce, oregano, pepper, and garlic powder. Add ground beef and onion, mixing well. Simmer. Drain fat from sausage, pat with towel to remove excess oil and fat. Place sausage in saucepan with tomato sauce and meat mixture. Continue simmering. DO NOT BOIL. Stir often.

Bring water, salt, and oil to boil in large pot. Add noodles, one at a time. Bring to a second boil, then follow cooking directions on package. While noodles are cooking, mix cottage cheese, parsley, and beaten egg in a bowl. Set aside. Remove sausage from sauce and cut into ¼-inch round slices. Stir sauce to avoid sticking. After sauce has cooked for 15 minutes (or when sausage is cooked thoroughly), remove from heat.

Drain noodles. Layer one half of the noodles in a lightly greased 9- by 13-inch baking dish spread with half of the cottage cheese mixture. Add half of the sausage slices, then half of the sauce and meat mixture; sprinkle half of the shredded or sliced mozzarella cheese. Repeat layers. Sprinkle Parmesan cheese on top. Bake for 30 to 35 minutes at 375 degrees.

Note: This recipe can be prepared in advance and refrigerated. Bake for 45 minutes to 1 hour. Wait a few minutes after baking, then slice and serve.

Makes 10 servings.

> This is a great main meal just for the family or for dinner guests. The only other dish you need with it is a tossed salad to make a complete meal. We use prepared tomato sauce because it's so good and saves time.

BEEF STROGANOFF

Senator Robert Byrd, WEST VIRGINIA

- 1½ pounds round steak
- ¼ cup butter
- 1 cup mushrooms, sliced
- 1 clove garlic, minced
- ½ cup onion, chopped
- 1¼ cups tomato soup
- 1 cup sour cream
- Salt to taste
- Pepper to taste

Cut beef into long thin strips. Brown beef in butter in a heavy skillet. Add mushrooms, garlic, and onion. Cook until lightly browned.

Blend in tomato soup, sour cream, salt, and pepper. Cover and simmer about 1 hour or until beef is tender. Stir occasionally. Serve with hot cooked rice.

Makes 6 servings.

LOUISIANA GRILLADES AND GRITS

Senator John Breaux, LOUISIANA

2½   pounds round steak

      Salt and pepper, or Tony Chachere's Creole seasoning

½   cup flour

3   tablespoons vegetable oil

3   tablespoons vermouth

2   large onions, coarsely chopped

1   large green pepper, coarsely chopped

½   cup celery, coarsely chopped

3   cloves garlic, minced

2   cups water

6   servings of grits

Pound the steak and cut into 2- by 3-inch pieces. Season with salt and pepper or Creole seasoning. Dredge meat in flour and shake off the excess. In a heavy skillet, heat oil and brown meat. Remove meat from skillet and set aside. Pour off remaining fat in skillet and add vermouth. Add onions, green pepper, celery, and garlic.

Cook for about 5 minutes, stirring frequently, or until the vegetables are tender. Stir in water and bring to a boil.

Return meat to pan and reduce heat to low. Cover and simmer for 1 hour or until meat is tender and gravy has been reduced to a thick sauce.

Adjust seasonings. Cook grits according to package directions. Mound grits on warm plates and ladle grillades and gravy over grits.

Makes 6 servings.

PASTA CARBONARA

Representative John Elias Baldacci, MAINE

¼ pound bacon
1 tablespoon butter
1 cup milk
2 tablespoons wine vinegar
1 pound pasta
2 eggs, whipped
⅓ cup Parmesan or Romano cheese

Cut bacon into little pieces and cook in butter until clear. Heat milk in a small saucepan and add the bacon and butter. Add wine vinegar. This will turn the milk to cheese. Simmer for about 15 minutes until the sauce cooks smooth.

Boil your favorite pasta in salted water. Drain and return to the pan. Immediately add whipped eggs, the prepared sauce, and freshly grated cheese. Season with salt and pepper. Toss and serve.

My family has owned and operated an Italian restaurant in Bangor, Maine, for many years. I grew up working in the restaurant with my brothers and sisters, and I learned the value of hard work and cooperation. I have been fortunate to have been able to put these qualities to good use in my service to Congress. This recipe is popular at our restaurant.

CHILES RELLENOS CASEROLE

Senator Ben Nighthorse Campbell, COLORADO

21 ounces whole green chilies or fresh Poblano chilies,
roasted, peeled, and seeded, stem intact and open flat

½ cup salsa

1 small yellow onion, diced

2 cups Monterey Jack cheese, shredded

2 cups cheddar cheese, shredded

4 to 6 corn tortillas, cut into wide strips

8 eggs

½ cup milk

½ teaspoon salt

½ teaspoon pepper

½ teaspoon garlic powder

½ teaspoon ground cumin

2 sprigs fresh cilantro

½ teaspoon paprika

Begin by covering the bottom of a well-greased 9-inch-square baking dish with chilies. Top with a layer of onions and a layer of cheese. Sprinkle lightly with salsa and a layer of tortilla strips. Repeat layers, beginning with chilies. Build to three layers.

Beat together eggs, milk, salt, pepper, garlic powder, and cumin. Stir in minced cilantro and paprika for color.

Pour mixture evenly over casserole. Bake uncovered at 350 degrees for about 40 minutes or until puffy and set in the center when lightly touched. Let stand about 10 minutes before serving.

Coming from southwestern Colorado, I am a big fan of Mexican food. One of my very favorites is Chiles Rellenos casserole.

SAUSAGE GRAVY AND BISCUITS

★

Representative Mike DeWine, OHIO

1 pound bulk sausage
½ cup flour
3 cups cold milk
  Salt to taste
  Pepper to taste
  Hot biscuits

Brown sausage in heavy skillet and remove to plate. Leave about ¼ cup of drippings and a few bits of sausage in skillet. Add flour, cooking and stirring over medium heat until bubbly. Add milk slowly, stirring over medium heat until thickened. Add browned sausage to gravy and heat. Serve over hot biscuits.

Makes 4 to 6 servings.

DUCK AND WILD RICE CASSEROLE

Representative Marion Berry, ARKANSAS

2 medium ducks (3 cups meat)
3 stalks celery
1 onion, halved
Salt to taste
Pepper to taste
6 ounces wild rice
6 ounces long grain rice
½ cup butter or margarine
½ cup onion, chopped
¼ cup flour
1 4-ounce can mushrooms, sliced
1½ cups half-and-half
1 tablespoon parsley
1½ teaspoons salt
¼ teaspoon pepper
Slivered almonds

Boil ducks for 1 hour in water with celery, onion halves, salt, and pepper. Remove meat and cube. Reserve broth. Cook rice according to package directions. Melt margarine, saute onions, and stir in flour. Drain mushrooms, reserving broth. Add mushrooms to the onion mixture. Add enough duck broth to the mushroom broth to make 1½ cups of liquid. Stir this into the onion mixture. Add half-and-half, parsley, salt, and pepper.

Place in greased 2-quart casserole dish. Sprinkle almonds on top. Bake covered at 350 degrees for 15 to 20 minutes. Uncover and bake for 5 to 10 minutes more. Chicken substituted for duck also makes a tasty dish.

ISLAND SAMOAN CHOP SUEY

Representative Eni Faleomavaega, SAMOA

1½ bundles bean-thread long rice noodles
1 pound meat (beef, pork, or chicken)
Garlic powder
Pepper
5 tablespoons olive oil
½ cup onion, chopped
2 or 3 garlic cloves, chopped
3 ounces gingerroot, chopped
12 ounces chicken or beef broth
3 cups mixed fresh or canned vegetables (chopped carrots, celery, green peppers, cabbage)
¼ cup Kikkoman Shoyu sauce
3 tablespoons sesame oil

Soak the strings of long rice in a bowl of hot water to soften. Season the meat, chopped into stir-fry size, with garlic powder and pepper in a bowl. Pour the oil in an 8-quart pot and add onions and garlic; heat until onions sizzle. Add meat. Stir and turn the meat until cooked; add the chopped ginger at the same time. Keep the mixture moist by adding broth to the pot.

Add the chopped vegetables. Drain the water from the bowl of long rice noodles and chop the strings into 4-inch lengths.

Add the Shoyu sauce and sesame oil and mix it all together. At the same time, add more broth to balance the juices and contents.

The heat should be medium high and reduced later to medium.

Good luck and enjoy!

GIOVANNI'S POLLO MARINATO

Representative Elton Gallegly, CALIFORNIA

 1 pound chicken breasts, boneless and skinned
 6 ounces white wine
 6 ounces olive oil
 1 lemon, juiced
 1 teaspoon salt
    Fresh basil
    Tarragon
    Dill
12 ounces penne pasta
 3 cups whipping cream
 3 ounces porcini mushrooms
 3 ounces sundried tomatoes
    Salt to taste
    Pepper to taste
    Parmesan cheese, grated

Marinate chicken breasts in wine, olive oil, lemon juice, and spices for 2 hours. Boil water for pasta and cook approximately 15 minutes. Slice chicken into thin strips and cook in the whipping cream.

When chicken appears almost done, add mushrooms, sundried tomatoes, and salt and pepper to taste. Toss with penne pasta and serve with grated Parmesan cheese on top.

This recipe is compliments of our favorite restaurant, Pastabilities.

MEATS

★ 6

Beef,
Pork,
Ham,
and Game

PORK CHOPS
WITH APPLES

Senator George Voinovich, OHIO

8 loin pork chops
Salt to taste
Pepper to taste
½ cup apple juice or cider
3 tablespoons ketchup
½ cup soy sauce
½ cup brown sugar
2 tablespoons cornstarch
½ teaspoon ground ginger
2 apples (we like Golden Delicious)

Bake chops with salt and pepper in roasting pan, uncovered for 30 minutes at 350 degrees. Turn chops over.

Combine juice, ketchup, soy sauce, brown sugar, cornstarch, and ginger. Cook over medium heat until thickened. Spoon some juice from roasting pan into sauce to thin.

Core apples; cut into rings and place one ring on each chop. Pour sauce over pork chops. Bake 30 minutes longer. Baste several times.

George likes this with rice and broccoli.

PORK PIE

★

Representative John Shimkus, ILLINOIS

- 1   pound bulk pork sausage
- 1   cup cooked ham, cubed
- ½   teaspoon ground sage
- ½   teaspoon pepper
- 1   cup green pepper, chopped
- ½   cup onion, chopped
- ½   cup celery, chopped
- 1   10½-ounce can cream of chicken soup
- 1   apple, sliced
     Grated Parmesan cheese
- 1   pie crust
     Butter or margarine

Cook and stir sausage in 10-inch skillet until done. Drain. Stir in ham, sage, pepper, green pepper, onion, celery, and cream of chicken soup. Place in ungreased deep-dish pie plate or quiche pan. Place sliced apples on top and sprinkle with cheese.

Cover with pie crust and seal. Prick pie crust and dot with butter or margarine. Bake at 375 degrees for 30 to 40 minutes.

Enjoy!

THAD COCHRAN'S FAVORITE MEAT LOAF

Senator Thad Cochran, MISSISSIPPI

1½ pounds ground beef
1 cup cracker crumbs
2 eggs, beaten
1 8-ounce can tomato sauce, with tomato bits
½ cup onion, finely chopped
2 tablespoons green pepper, chopped
1 medium-sized bay leaf, crushed
1 teaspoon thyme leaves, dried
1 teaspoon marjoram leaves, dried

Preheat oven to 350 degrees. Mix ingredients thoroughly. Place in lightly greased loaf pan. Bake for 1 hour.

SENATOR BYRD'S FAVORITE CABBAGE ROLLS

★

Senator Robert Byrd, WEST VIRGINIA

1	pound lean ground beef
1	cup cooked white rice
1	small onion, chopped
1	teaspoon salt
¼	teaspoon pepper
1	egg
10	cabbage leaves
1	tablespoon vegetable oil
1	16-ounce can tomato sauce
¼	cup water

Mix ground beef, cooked rice, chopped onion, salt, pepper, and egg together. Trim off thickest part of stem from cabbage leaves. Divide meat into equal portions, wrap each in a leaf, and fasten with wooden picks.

Brown cabbage rolls slightly in oil. Add tomato sauce and water to pan. Cover and cook slowly for about 40 minutes.

PHILIP CRANE'S FAVORITE HAM LOAF

★

Representative Philip Crane, ILLINOIS

LOAF:

    2   pounds ground ham
    1   pound ground fresh pork
    2   eggs
    1½ cups cracker crumbs
    1   cup milk
        Garlic to taste

TOPPING AND GARNISH:

    1½ cups brown sugar, packed
    1½ teaspoons dry mustard
    1   10½-ounce can tomato soup
    ¼   cup raisins and/or pineapple for garnish

Mix all ham loaf ingredients together well. Shape into loaf in pan.

To prepare topping, mix together sugar, mustard, and soup. Pour topping over loaf.

Garnish with raisins and/or pineapple, if desired.

Bake ham loaf in preheated 350-degree oven for 1½ hours.

MEATS   143

LITE-AND-LEAN
BEEF BROIL

★

Representative Larry Craig, IDAHO

½ cup soy sauce

¼ cup water

2 tablespoons lemon juice

2 tablespoons honey

1 teaspoon instant minced onion

¼ teaspoon garlic powder

1½ pounds sirloin, top round, or flank steak

2 tablespoons sesame seeds

Combine marinade ingredients in nonmetal pan. Add beef and turn to coat. Marinate beef for 24 to 48 hours in refrigerator.

Broil beef to desired doneness (do not overcook; best served medium-rare).

To serve, slice beef across the grain into thin slices. Sprinkle with sesame seeds.

Makes 4 to 6 servings.

MOOSE SWISS STEAK

Representative Don Young, ALASKA

        3   pounds moose steak
        2   tablespoons lemon juice
       ¼   cup flour
        1   teaspoon dry mustard
     1½   teaspoons salt
       ¼   teaspoon pepper
       ⅓   cup shortening
        1   small onion, sliced
    14½   ounces canned tomatoes

Sprinkle meat with lemon juice and pierce with fork to tenderize. Mix dry ingredients together and add meat to mixture.

Brown meat slowly in shortening. Place in a 2-quart casserole dish and cover with sliced onions and tomatoes.

Bake at 325 degrees for 1½ to 2 hours.

Makes 6 servings.

An Alaskan favorite!

MANDARIN PORK STEAKS

Senator Christopher Bond, MISSOURI

1	beef bouillon cube
⅓	cup hot water
1	teaspoon ground ginger
2	teaspoons salt
1	tablespoon sugar
¼	cup honey
¼	cup soy sauce
4 to 6	pork arm or blade steaks

Place bouillon and water in a large glass, stainless steel, or enamel-ware pan. Stir until dissolved. Add all ingredients except pork. Mix well. Add pork.

Refrigerate at least 2 hours, preferably overnight, turning occasionally.

Preheat oven to 350 degrees or prepare outdoor grill. Remove pork steaks from marinade and place on rack in shallow roasting pan.

Bake for 50 minutes or until done, or grill 4 inches from coals 12 to 15 minutes on each side or until juices run clear. Baste each side frequently with marinade.

Makes 4 to 6 servings.

TERIYAKI BEEF

Senator Tim Johnson, SOUTH DAKOTA

1¼   cups brown sugar

1   cup soy sauce

½   teaspoon ginger, grated

½   garlic clove, crushed

⅛   teaspoon sesame oil

2 or 3   pounds flank steak or 4 small ¾-inch thick steaks

Combine sugar, soy sauce, ginger, garlic, and oil, stirring well. Pour over steak and marinate 3 hours, turning meat occasionally. Broil or barbecue to taste.

Makes 4 servings.

ELK STEW

Representative Randy "Duke" Cunningham, CALIFORNIA

4 slices bacon, halved
1½ pounds elk or beef chuck steak, trimmed and cubed
1 quart plus ½ cup water
1¼ cup onions, chopped
2 bay leaves
1 teaspoon salt
3 potatoes, peeled and diced
2 carrots, peeled and diced
1 large turnip, diced
¼ cup acorn meal or hazelnuts finely ground

In a large skillet over medium heat, cook bacon until some of its fat is rendered. Add elk and brown with the bacon. Add 1 quart water, onion, bay leaves, and salt.

Cover and simmer for 1½ hours. Add potatoes, carrot, and turnip and cook 30 minutes longer. Combine remaining water with acorn meal and stir into the simmering stew. Cover tightly and steam 12 to 15 minutes.

I am honored to contribute to the fight for literacy.

NEBRASKA BEEF BRISKET

★

Senator Ben Nelson, NEBRASKA

1   Nebraska beef brisket
1   large onion, sliced
2   teaspoons liquid smoke
    Salt to taste
    Pepper to taste

Rub a good cut of Nebraska beef brisket with your favorite spices. Add liquid smoke, sliced onions, and salt and pepper.

Wrap tightly in foil and place in a shallow 9- by 13-inch baking pan.

Bake at 250 degrees for 6 hours. Let sit for 10 minutes before slicing or shredding.

PRIME RIB

Senator Ben Nelson, NEBRASKA

5 pounds Nebraska prime rib roast, boned
2 teaspoons Kitchen Bouquet
Salt to taste
Pepper to taste
Whole garlic cloves

Rub roast with Kitchen Bouquet and salt and pepper. Arrange in shallow baking pan with whole garlic cloves and more Kitchen Bouquet.

Bake covered at 425 degrees for 1 hour. Turn oven down to 200 degrees. Cook for another 1 to 1½ hours. Meat thermometer should read 130 degrees.

Let sit for 10 minutes before carving. Serve with creamy horseradish sauce or mushroom sauce.

PORK ROAST IN MUSTARD SAUCE

Senator Jon Kyl, ARIZONA

1   4-pound boneless pork loin
½   teaspoon salt
    Freshly ground pepper
¼   teaspoon garlic powder
⅓   cup Dijon mustard
⅓   cup vinegar
2   cups cream
2   tablespoons Dijon mustard
2   tablespoons cold butter
    Salt to taste

Trim excess fat from roast. Sprinkle roast with salt, pepper, and garlic powder. Spread ⅓ cup mustard over roast and place in large Dutch oven. Cover and bake for 3 hours at 325 degrees or until meat thermometer reads 170 degrees. Remove roast and set aside to keep warm. Add vinegar and freshly ground pepper to pan. Boil mixture, scraping bottom of pan.

Cook mixture until it is reduced in volume by half. Stir in cream; simmer for 5 minutes. Remove from heat; stir in 2 tablespoons mustard, butter, and salt to taste. Spoon half of hot sauce over sliced pork roast and serve with remaining sauce.

Note: I usually prepare half of this recipe when serving my family. It is very easy and very tender, and leftovers reheat well. It is 3½ hours to prepare and not suitable for freezing.

Serves 12 to 14.

QUICK AND EASY TACO MEATBALLS

★

Senator Conrad Burns, MONTANA

2 pounds ground beef
½ onion, chopped
2 eggs, slightly beaten
1 package taco mix
   Salt to taste
   Pepper to taste
   Garlic salt to taste

Mix ingredients together. Form into small meatballs and place on cookie sheet. Bake at 400 degrees for 15 minutes.
Makes 6 to 8 servings.

This is a great and easy dish!

IOWA CHOPS

★

Senator Tom Harkin, IOWA

   2   Iowa pork chops

STUFFING:
- ½ cup whole-kernel corn
- ½ cup bread crumbs
- Pinch of salt
- Pinch of pepper
- ¾ tablespoon parsley
- Pinch of sage
- ½ tablespoon onion, chopped
- ½ cup apple, diced
- 1 tablespoon whole milk

BASTING SAUCE:
- ¼ cup mustard
- ¼ cup honey
- ½ teaspoon salt
- ¼ teaspoon rosemary
- Pinch of pepper

Cut pocket into side of chops. Combine stuffing ingredients and stuff chops. Brown in pan, then bake at 350 degrees for about 1 hour. Baste often with basting sauce mixture.

Makes 2 servings.

BEEF STROGANOFF

Representative John Linder, GEORGIA

Sirloin steak, cut in cubes
¼ pound butter
1 onion, minced
1 green pepper, diced
Salt to taste
Pepper to taste
1 tablespoon Worcestershire sauce
1 tablespoon garlic powder
1 cup mushrooms, sliced
Dash of Tabasco sauce
2 tablespoons red wine vinegar
1 pint sour cream
1 cup heavy cream

Cook steak cubes in butter. Add onion and green pepper; cook until soft. Add remaining ingredients.

POULTRY AND SEAFOOD

★ 7

Chicken,
Duck,
Shellfish,
and Fish

CHICKEN FLORENTINE

Vice President Dick Cheney

2 packages (10 ounces each) frozen, chopped spinach
1 clove, garlic, crushed and minced
¼ cup butter
Dash ground thyme
Dash ground basil
⅓ cup half-and-half
¼ cup all-purpose flour
5 cups cooked chicken, sliced
¾ cup half-and-half
¾ cup chicken broth
Salt to taste
Pepper to taste
6 thin slices ham
1¼ cup grated Parmesan cheese

Cook spinach according to package instructions, drain well. In a skillet, melt 1 tablespoon butter; add minced garlic, basil, and thyme. Cook over medium heat, stirring constantly, for about 5 minutes. Put spinach into the bottom of a lightly buttered 2-quart casserole or baking dish. Cover with cooked chicken slices.

Over medium low heat, melt the remaining butter and blend in remaining flour, stirring until smooth. Gradually stir in ¾ cup half-and-half and ¾ cup chicken broth; continue cooking and stirring until thickened. Season to taste with salt and pepper. Cut sliced ham in strips. Add to sauce and pour over chicken.

Cover all with grated Parmesan cheese. Bake at 400 degrees for 20 minutes or until cheese is lightly browned.

Serves 6.

DOVE ON THE GRILL

Senator Richard Shelby, ALABAMA

Dove (allow at least 2 per person)
Salt to taste
Pepper to taste
Worcestershire sauce to taste
Bacon (1 slice per bird)

Sprinkle dove with salt, pepper, and Worcestershire sauce. Wrap each dove with bacon. Secure with toothpick if necessary.

Cook over a medium fire until done, about 20 to 30 minutes. Turn occasionally.

Variation: Wrap ½ strip of bacon around a water chestnut and a boneless dove breast. Season lemon butter with Worcestershire sauce and baste frequently. Cook on grill or broil until bacon is done.

KOREAN CHICKEN

Senator Daniel Akaka, HAWAII

5 pounds chicken
1 tablespoon salt
1 cup flour
2 tablespoons vegetable oil

SAUCE:
1 scallion, chopped
1 small red pepper, chopped
1 clove garlic, chopped
6 tablespoons sugar
½ cup soy sauce
1 teaspoon sesame oil

Clean chicken and salt. Let chicken stand overnight in refrigerator. Roll chicken in flour and fry in oil.

After frying, mix sauce ingredients. Dip chicken in sauce and serve.

SAXBY'S QUAIL

Senator Saxby Chambliss, GEORGIA

10 quail
   Salt and pepper
16 ounces butter
 1 tablespoon flour
 2 tablespoons Worcestershire sauce
 2 tablespoons lemon juice
 2 cups water
 1 cup fresh mushrooms, sliced

Salt and pepper the quail. Melt the butter and add the flour, Worcestershire sauce, lemon juice, and water. Bring to a boil.

Pour this mixture over the birds and add mushrooms. Bake in a covered baking dish for 2 hours at 350 degrees. This is wonderful with grits. Not suitable for freezing.

I hope that others will enjoy this!

POPPY SEED CHICKEN

Representative Roger Wicker, MISSISSIPPI

6 chicken breasts
1 10½-ounce can cream of mushroom soup
4 ounces sour cream
4 ounces margarine
1 cup Ritz crackers, crushed
1 tablespoon poppy seeds

Cook chicken; skin and debone. Place chopped chicken in buttered 9- by 13-inch casserole dish. Mix soup and sour cream. Spread over chicken.

Melt margarine. Mix with crushed crackers. Add poppy seeds and spread on top of casserole. Bake for 30 minutes at 30 degrees. Serve over rice.

Makes 6 servings.

CROCK-POT CORNISH HENS

★

Senator Don Nickles, OKLAHOMA

1   18-ounce package cornbread stuffing
3   Cornish hens, rinsed and patted dry
¼   cup butter, melted
2   tablespoons light brown sugar, packed
2   tablespoons lime juice
2   tablespoons dry white wine
2   tablespoons soy sauce

Prepare cornbread stuffing as directed on package. Stuff hens. Combine all remaining ingredients until well mixed. Brush sauce on hens. Arrange hens in Crock-Pot, neck down. Cover and cook hens on low setting for 5 to 7 hours, occasionally basting with sauce.

P. A.'S BAKED SHRIMP

Representative Trent Lott, MISSISSIPPI

     5 pounds medium to large shrimp, heads off but in shells
½ to 1 small bottle Worcestershire sauce
     1 tablespoon salt
     1 21-ounce bottle ketchup
     1 teaspoon horseradish
     1 lemon, juiced

Wash shrimp and drain. Place in oblong noncorrosive baking dish. Mix all ingredients and pour over shrimp, stirring every 15 to 20 minutes. Do not cover.

Bake in preheated 350-degree oven for 1 hour or until shrimp begin to pull away from shells. Guests peel their own shrimp.

Note: Peel shrimp by pulling tail off, then grabbing legs and pulling off the shell in one round motion.

Makes 8 servings.

RED SPANISH SCAMPI PROVENCALE

Representative Henry J. Hyde, ILLINOIS

8 jumbo Red Spanish shrimp
½ cup flour
  Salt to taste
  White pepper to taste
3 or 4 tablespoons clarified butter
3 ripe tomatoes, peeled and chopped
6 tablespoons butter
1 tablespoon fresh parsley, chopped
½ clove garlic, chopped

Clean, devein, and butterfly shrimp. Dust with flour. Season with salt and pepper. In a pan large enough to hold shrimp without crowding, heat clarified butter. Gently cook shrimp over moderate heat until nicely golden.

Add chopped tomatoes and cook for approximately 3 minutes. Remove from heat and add butter, parsley, and garlic. Heat pan and its ingredients over high heat until all the butter has been incorporated into tomatoes.

Serve dish along with boiled potatoes.

MEXICANA CHICKEN

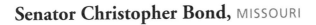

Senator Christopher Bond, MISSOURI

1 10¾-ounce can cream of chicken soup
1 10¾-ounce can cream of celery soup
1 10½-ounce can chicken broth
1 4-ounce can green chilies
12 corn tortillas, broken into small pieces
3 cups cooked chicken, chopped
8 ounces cheddar cheese, chopped

Combine soups, broth, chilies, and tortillas. Let stand 30 minutes. Preheat oven to 350 degrees. Place half of the mixture in a greased 9- by 13-inch baking dish. Cover with chicken. Pour remaining mixture over chicken and sprinkle with cheese. Bake uncovered for 25 minutes.

Makes 8 to 10 servings.

COCO'S SHRIMP
AND RICE

★

Representative Porter Goss, FLORIDA

½   cup butter, melted
1   pint cream
4   tablespoons Worcestershire sauce
½   teaspoon Tabasco sauce
2   tablespoons ketchup
2   cups cooked rice
2   cups cooked shrimp

Combine all ingredients and bake at 350 degrees for approximately 1 hour.

Makes 4 to 6 servings.

Easy and elegant!

NORFOLK CRAB CAKES

Senator John Warner, VIRGINIA

2   fresh onions, chopped (preferably two types for a variety of flavor and texture)

2   green peppers, chopped

1   pound fresh Chesapeake Bay blue crabmeat

2   eggs

½   cup bread crumbs

    Pepper to taste

½   teaspoon salt

¼   cup heavy cream

2   tablespoons butter

2   tablespoons parsley

Precook onion, taking care not to lose firmness of texture. Lightly saute green pepper to release full flavor. Mix crab, onions, green pepper, eggs, bread crumbs, pepper, and small amount of salt (crabmeat is naturally slightly salty). Add a touch of cream.

Saute butter until brown and quickly add parsley to release parsley's natural flavor. Form cakes and drop in butter, cooking sparingly so as not to lose the enhanced fresh crab flavor. Remove and serve.

> This is a creative recipe and the precise measurements, preparation of the mix, and cooking variables are trade secrets known only to the chef! Traditional crab cakes are those made with a mix of the ingredients recommended above and the amounts to suit the chef's particular taste.

SUPER FISH

★

Senator Chuck Grassley, IOWA

3	pounds frozen haddock or cod fillets
	Salt to taste
2 to 3	tablespoons onion, minced
2	tablespoons butter
1	cup sour cream
1	10½-ounce can cream of mushroom soup
1	10½-ounce can cream of celery soup
1	tablespoon parsley

Thaw fish and place in 8- by 12-inch baking dish, still in block size. Sprinkle with salt. Saute onion in butter.

Mix all other ingredients except parsley and heat together. Pour over fish and bake for 30 to 40 minutes at 375 degrees or until fish is done. Sprinkle with parsley before baking or put fresh parsley on top a few minutes before finished baking.

Makes 6 to 8 servings.

This is another of my mother's creations. She cooks it in the microwave these days!

FILLET OF SOLE

Representative Richard Gephardt, MISSOURI

¼ cup green onions, chopped
3 pounds sole or flounder
   Salt to taste
   Pepper to taste
¾ cup white wine
1½ cups water
4 tablespoons butter
¼ cup flour
¾ cup milk
2 egg yolks
¼ cup cream
1 teaspoon lemon juice
¾ pound shrimp
3 tablespoons Swiss cheese, grated

Preheat oven to 350 degrees. Butter bottom of shallow baking dish. Sprinkle with chopped green onion. Lay fillets over onion. Season with salt and pepper. Pour in white wine and water to come almost to top of fish. Bring to slow simmer on stove. Cover dish and bake in oven for 10 minutes. Drain off liquid and save for sauce.

In a 2-quart pan, melt the butter. Stir in flour slowly, and continue stirring for 1 to 2 minutes. Remove from heat and add poaching liquid and milk. Return to high heat and stir until it thickens and comes to a boil.

Let simmer for 1 minute. Mix egg yolks with the cream. Stir in 2 tablespoons of hot mixture and then 2 more. Add egg and cream mixture to hot sauce and bring to a boil over moderate heat. Boil for 30 seconds. Remove from heat.

Add 1 or 2 drops of lemon juice, and salt and pepper to taste. Sauce should lightly coat spoon. If more liquid has accumulated in baking dish, add to sauce. Cover sole with shrimp and then sauce and Swiss cheese. Bake at 425 degrees in top third of oven for 10 to 15 minutes or until sauce bubbles.

Makes 6 servings.

BROILED SWORDFISH

★

Senator John Chafee, RHODE ISLAND

4 pounds skinless, boneless swordfish
1 medium onion, chopped
   Pinch of dried thyme
   Pinch of dried tarragon
1 bay leaf
1 lemon, juiced
   Corn oil
4 medium green peppers
1 pound fresh button mushrooms
   Butter
   Lemon juice
   Salt to taste
   Pepper to taste

Cut swordfish into cubes, approximately 2 ounces each (4 cubes per person). Place cubes in a bowl and add onion, thyme, tarragon, bay leaf, and lemon juice. Cover with corn oil and marinate in refrigerator overnight.

Cut green pepper into quarters and remove seeds. Boil green pepper quarters for 5 minutes. Drain. Saute mushroom caps in butter with a drop of lemon juice for 5 minutes. Remove swordfish cubes from oil and place on skews, alternating with mushrooms and green peppers. Sprinkle with salt and pepper and broil for 15 minutes, turning frequently. Serve on rice.

Makes 6 to 8 servings.

FISH NEAPOLITAN

Senator John Breaux, LOUISIANA

3   tablespoons vermouth
1   onion, chopped
¼   green pepper, chopped
2   tablespoons parsley, chopped
3   medium tomatoes, cut in pieces
½   cup tomato juice
½   teaspoon basil
⅛   teaspoon pepper
1   pound fish fillets (sea bass, snapper, or perch)

Heat vermouth in large frying pan and cook onions 2 to 3 minutes. Add rest of ingredients except fish. Simmer until tomatoes and peppers are soft, or about 10 minutes. Add fish and simmer until fish flakes.

Makes 4 servings.

Great low-cal meal!

CAJUN DEEP-FRIED TURKEY

★

Senator John Breaux, LOUISIANA

4   ounces liquid garlic
4   ounces liquid onion
4   ounces liquid celery
1   tablespoon red pepper
2   tablespoons salt
2   tablespoons Tabasco sauce
1   ounce liquid crab boil or 1 tablespoon Old Bay Seasoning
1   poultry or meat injector
1   10 to 12 pound turkey, defrosted
4   gallons peanut oil

Saute first 7 ingredients until salt and pepper are dissolved. Fill the injector with first 7 ingredients and inject turkey at breast, wings, drumsticks, thighs, and back. Allow to marinate 24 hours in refrigerator or ice chest.

Use a 10-gallon pot for frying. Bring peanut oil to 350-degree temperature and fry turkey for 38 to 44 minutes. Turkey should float to surface after 35 minutes and you should cook an additional 5 to 7 minutes.

> You may want to tie turkey legs with ½-inch cotton ropes to be able to remove from frying pot when done. The cooking of fried turkey should be done outdoors. Extreme caution should be taken when placing cold turkey in hot oil.

CHICKEN BREASTS IN PAPRIKA CREAM SAUCE

Senator Harry Reid, NEVADA

½   cup onions, finely chopped
½   cup butter
1   tablespoon paprika
4   chicken breasts, deboned
¼   cup white wine
¼   cup chicken stock
1   cup heavy cream
     Salt to taste
     Pepper to taste
1   teaspoon lemon juice

Boil onions 3 to 4 minutes. Drain well. Melt butter in casserole dish over low heat. Then add onions, but do not brown. Add paprika and remove from heat. Roll chicken breasts in mixture and bake covered at 350 degrees until chicken breasts are done. Remove from oven and set aside.

Heat sauce mixture of wine and chicken stock. Bring to a boil and let cook for 3 to 4 minutes. Remove from heat. Add cream and stir well. Cook over low heat for 2 to 3 minutes. Add salt, pepper, and lemon juice to taste. Pour this mixture over baked chicken breasts. Serve with garnish.

Makes 4 servings.

Tasty and delicious with potatoes or rice!

WILD DUCK

Senator Pete Domenici, NEW MEXICO

6 wild ducks, preferably from New Mexico skies
   Salt and pepper
3 apples, cut in wedges
3 onions, 2 cut in wedges and 1 finely diced
3 packages dry brown gravy mix
½ cup flour
2 teaspoons salt
6 tablespoons lemon juice
12 ounces frozen orange juice, undiluted
6 tablespoons orange marmalade
¾ cup white wine (optional)
1½ cups hot water
3 oven cooking bags
7 cups wild rice, cooked

Thoroughly wash ducks. Wipe dry inside and out. Sprinkle duck cavities with salt and pepper. Place an apple and an onion wedge in each duck.

Combine gravy mix, flour, salt, lemon and orange juices, marmalade, white wine, diced onion, and hot water. Arrange 2 ducks in each cooking bag. Divide liquid mixture among the 3 bags and seal each according to instructions. Place in roasting pan and cut 2 or 3 slits in top of each bag. Bake at 350 degrees for 2½ hours. Serve ducks with pan gravy and wild rice.

Makes 12 to 14 servings.

IMPERIAL CRAB

Senator Barbara Mikulski, MARYLAND

1 pound backfin crabmeat
Dash of salt
Dash of cayenne pepper
1 green pepper, diced
2 eggs, well beaten (set aside 2 tablespoons)
5 tablespoons mayonnaise, divided
1 tablespoon onion, chopped

Pick over crabmeat. Combine with salt, cayenne pepper, green pepper, beaten eggs, 4 tablespoons mayonnaise, and chopped onion. Fill 6 decorative serving shells with crabmeat mixture. Add 1 tablespoon mayonnaise to remaining egg and put over each filled shell. Dot with cayenne pepper. Bake at 350 degrees for about 30 minutes.

Makes 6 servings.

ALASKAN MARINATED GRILLED SALMON

★

Senator Ted Stevens, ALASKA

1 cup liquid brown sugar
1 cup dry white wine
1 cup soy sauce
1 onion, sliced
3 cloves garlic, diced
1 9-pound salmon, butterflied with backbone removed

Combine first 5 ingredients and pour over salmon. Refrigerate 3 hours to overnight, turning occasionally. Place salmon skin-side down on aluminum foil and place on grill. Grill over medium-hot charcoal or mesquite. Test frequently for doneness for 30 minutes or until salmon loses its translucence.

Makes 15 servings.

HONEY MUSTARD CHICKEN

Senator Frank R. Lautenberg, NEW JERSEY

4 to 6   chicken breasts, skinless and boneless
½   cup butter or margarine, melted
½   cup honey
¼   cup Dijon mustard
    Salt to taste
    Pepper to taste

Preheat oven to 350 degrees. Mix together butter or margarine, honey, mustard, salt, and pepper. Pour over chicken pieces.

Bake uncovered for approximately 45 minutes or until done, basting often.

Serve with rice or couscous.

SESAME CHICKEN

Senator John Ensign, NEVADA

2 pounds chicken breasts or chicken tenders
1 egg
2 tablespoons flour
2 tablespoons cornstarch
2 tablespoons water
1 teaspoon salt
2 teaspoons vegetable oil
¼ teaspoon baking soda
¼ teaspoon white pepper
½ cup water
¼ cup cornstarch
1 cup sugar
1 cup chicken broth
¾ cup rice vinegar
2 teaspoons soy sauce
2 teaspoons chili paste
1 teaspoon vegetable oil
1 clove garlic, finely chopped
2 tablespoons sesame seeds, toasted
Fruit added to sauce (optional)

This is so yummy and my kids love it!

Cut chicken into 2½-inch strips. Mix next 8 ingredients and stir chicken into mixture. Cover and refrigerate 20 minutes. Mix water and cornstarch and set aside. Heat next 7 ingredients and cook to boiling. Stir in the cornstarch mixture. Cook and stir until thickened.

Remove from heat, but keep warm. Heat 1½ inches of oil to 350 degrees. Fry chicken, adding one at a time for 3 minutes or until light brown. Remove chicken with a slotted spoon and drain on paper towels.

Place chicken on heated platter. Heat sauce to boiling and pour over chicken. Sprinkle with sesame seeds. Serve with white rice.

HOT SEAFOOD SALAD

Representative Dennis Hastert, ILLINOIS

5 pounds crabmeat, flaked
2 bunches green onions, finely chopped
½ cup lemon juice
2 teaspoons tarragon, crushed
5 tablespoons capers
2 cups mayonnaise
2 tablespoons horseradish
3 teaspoons Dijon mustard
Salt to taste
Pepper to taste
Bread crumbs, seasoned
Melted butter
Parsley, chopped
Parmesan cheese, grated
Pitas
Mustard

Mix first 10 ingredients together. Spoon into buttered individual baking dishes. Mix bread crumbs, butter, and parsley. Sprinkle crumbs and Parmesan cheese on crab mixture. Bake at 350 degrees about 20 minutes. Serve hot with pita crackers. Makes 20 servings.

Pita crackers: Cut each pita circle in half and separate each half into 2 pieces where pocket is formed. Brush both sides with mixture of butter and mustard. Bake at 350 degrees until brown. Serve hot with salad.

PACIFIC SALMON

★

Representative Norm Dicks, WASHINGTON

Pacific salmon, smoked
Crackers
Capers
Cream cheese
Chopped onion

Catch Pacific salmon. Have salmon smoked and vacuum-packed in individual serving sizes. Salmon may be frozen up to 6 months. Serve salmon sliced with crackers, capers, cream cheese, and chopped onions.

GOVERNOR'S FISH IN COCONUT MILK

Representative Madeleine Z. Bordallo, GUAM

2 pounds fish (skipjack, mullet, dolphin, or island fish),
  sliced about 2 inches thick
½ onion, sliced
¼ cup vinegar
½ cup water
1 clove garlic, mashed
1 green pepper, sliced
  Salt to taste
  Pepper to taste
1½ cups thick coconut milk

Put all ingredients in a pot except coconut milk and cook for about 20 minutes on medium heat or until the fish is cooked.

Add coconut milk last. Remove from direct heat. Do not boil coconut milk.

Serve hot with steamed rice.

KADON MANOK (CHICKEN STEW)

Representative Madeleine Z. Bordallo, GUAM

½ medium onion, chopped
2 tablespoons cooking oil
1 chicken, cut up
   Salt to taste
   Pepper to taste
8 medium Chinese cabbage leaves, cut into 1½-inch pieces

In a 3-quart saucepan, saute onions in oil. Add chicken, and salt and pepper to taste. Cover pan and reduce to medium heat.

Steam chicken until most of the juice is gone. Then add enough water to cover the chicken and cook until done.

Add Chinese cabbage to boiling broth and cook about 5 minutes.

Serve hot over rice.

GREAT BARBECUED KENAI SALMON

★

Senator Lisa Murkowski, ALASKA

½ cup apple cider
6   tablespoons soy sauce
2   tablespoons butter
1   large garlic clove, crushed
2   salmon fillets, each 2⅓ to 3 pounds;
    or a 4- to 5-pound salmon steak, cut 1-inch thick

Prepare a marinade by combining cider and soy sauce. Bring to a boil and reduce heat. Simmer 3 minutes. Add butter and garlic and continue cooking. Simmer, stirring occasionally, until liquid reduces and thickens enough to coat back of a spoon, about 20 minutes. Cool.

Brush marinade over salmon fillets and place skin side down on rack. Let stand 30 minutes at room temperature. Cook on hot coals; make an aluminum foil tent over fish. Bake for 15 to 20 minutes, until fish is tender and flakes.

There is nothing better than fresh Alaskan salmon!

BREADS

★ **8**

Yeast Breads,
Quick Breads,
Pancakes, and
Muffins

VIRGINIA BROWN BREAD

Representative Rick Boucher, VIRGINIA

1 cup brown sugar, packed

1 cup dark molasses

3 packages active dry yeast

2 tablespoons salt

2 cups nonfat dry milk powder

7 cups very warm water

5 tablespoons melted butter or margarine

3 eggs, lightly beaten

9 cups whole wheat flour

Approximately 8 cups white flour

Mix together all ingredients except white flour and let stand for 15 minutes. Work in enough white flour to make elastic, slightly sticky dough. Knead for several minutes.

Cover and let rise until double in bulk. Punch down dough and let rise again. Shape into 5 loaves and let rise in greased loaf pans until more than double.

Bake in preheated 350-degree oven until done, about 40 minutes. Makes 5 loaves.

> Southwest Virginia brown bread is a traditional favorite in the Fightin' Ninth congressional district of Virginia!

BUTTERHORN ROLLS

Representative Richard Gephardt, MISSOURI

1 fresh cake yeast or active dry yeast

1 cup lukewarm water

½ cup sugar

3 eggs, well beaten

¾ cup butter, melted

½ teaspoon salt

4 cups flour

Dissolve yeast in water. Add sugar, eggs, butter, and salt. Work in flour, mixing well. Cover dough and refrigerate overnight.

Divide dough into thirds. Shape each third into a ball. Roll out ball into circle ¼-inch thick. Cut dough (as if cutting a pie) into wedges. Starting from wider end roll up wedges to form rolls. Transfer to baking sheet; let rise 2 hours. Bake in preheated 400-degree oven about 15 minutes.

Makes about 2 dozen rolls.

Note: Since cake yeast is sometimes difficult to find, it may be more convenient to use a package of active dry yeast.

This recipe has been used through all the generations in our family and now, my son, Richard, bakes these rolls for many of his dinners when he and his wife, Jane, entertain.
—Loreen Gephardt

MARY'S SPOON BREAD

Senator Jim Bunning, KENTUCKY

1 cup cornmeal

2 cups milk, scalded

½ teaspoon salt

1 tablespoon sugar

1 cup margarine

5 eggs, separated

1½ tablespoons bourbon

Add cornmeal to scalded milk. Continue cooking and stirring until thick. Add salt, sugar, and margarine. Heat until margarine is melted. Add beaten egg yolks to mixture.

Fold in egg whites (beaten until stiff) and add bourbon. Bake in a 2-quart, greased casserole for 40 minutes at 350 degrees. Serve immediately.

Makes 6 to 8 servings.

CHERRY NUT BREAD

Senator Tim Johnson, SOUTH DAKOTA

   1   8-ounce package cream cheese
   1   cup margarine
   ½   cup sugar
   ½   teaspoon vanilla
   4   eggs
   2¼ cups flour, divided
   1½ teaspoons baking powder
   ¾   cup cherries
   ½   cup pecans, chopped

Thoroughly blend cream cheese, margarine, sugar, and vanilla. Add eggs one at a time, mixing well after each addition. Gradually add 2 cups flour sifted with baking powder. Combine remaining flour with cherries and nuts. Fold in batter.

Grease 10-inch loaf or Bundt pan and pour batter into pan. Bake at 325 degrees for 1 hour and 20 minutes. Cool 5 minutes, and remove from pan.

Glaze: Combine 1½ cups powdered sugar and 2 tablespoons milk, and then drizzle over cake.

SUNFLOWER WHEAT BREAD

Senator Kent Conrad, NORTH DAKOTA

1½ cups whole wheat flour

1 cup white flour

½ cup quick-cooking rolled oats

½ cup brown sugar, packed

1 tablespoon orange peel, finely shredded

½ teaspoon baking powder

½ teaspoon baking soda

½ teaspoon salt

1¾ cup buttermilk

1 egg, beaten

½ cup sunflower seeds

2 tablespoons honey, garnish

2 tablespoons sunflower kernels, garnish

In a large bowl, combine whole wheat flour, white flour, oats, sugar, orange peel, baking powder, baking soda, and salt until well blended. Add milk and egg; stir just until ingredients are moistened. Stir in sunflower seeds.

Pour into greased 9- by 5-inch bread pan. Bake at 350 degrees for 50 to 60 minutes or until bread tests done. If necessary, cover loaf with foil during the last 15 minutes of baking to prevent overbrowning.

Cool in pan for 10 minutes; turn out on a wire rack and allow to thoroughly cool before cutting. Brush top of loaf with honey and sprinkle with additional sunflower kernels, if desired.

Makes 1 loaf, or 16 slices.

ZUCCHINI BREAD

Representative Dave Weldon, FLORIDA

3 eggs, beaten
1 cup sugar
1 cup brown sugar
1 cup salad oil
2 cups zucchini, grated
1½ cups flour, sifted
¼ teaspoon baking soda
1 teaspoon salt
2½ teaspoons cinnamon
1 teaspoon vanilla
1 cup pecans, chopped (optional)

Beat eggs; add sugars, oil, and zucchini. Sift dry ingredients together and add to mixture; add vanilla and nuts. Pour into greased and floured 8- by 4- by 2-inch pans. (Small tins make 3 loaves.) Bake for 1 hour at 350 degrees.

I grew up in a working-class home with an Italian heritage. My mother was a school teacher and my father a postal employee. I never believed we were poor, but I was aware that my family had to operate within a budget. We didn't always have money left over at the end of the month for much beyond the basics. Our menus were often given variety, not by expensive ingredients, but by creative use of plentiful, common, and inexpensive ingredients—like the zucchini in this tasty recipe for a dessert bread. I may have been skeptical the first time I had "vegetable bread," but the spicy odor and margarine-melting warmth won me over. My parents made it clear I would have to pay my own way if I ever expected to make it through college, but I never considered that a "guarantee" anyway. To the contrary, I have always been grateful for the many valuable "inheritances" my parents left me: a strong work ethic, a high regard for family, and a faith in God. Recipes like this one are "icing on the cake" of that heritage.

BANANA NUT BREAD

Representative Chris Cannon, UTAH

2 cups sugar

3 cups flour

1 cup salad oil

2½ teaspoons baking soda

1 cup walnuts

5 eggs

1 teaspoon vanilla

1 teaspoon salt

7 to 10 ripe bananas, mashed

Mix ingredients together thoroughly. Bake for 1 hour in a greased and floured loaf pan at 325 or 350 degrees.

Makes 3 loaves.

Spectacular aroma in the kitchen.

WHOLE-MEAL IRISH SODA BREAD

Representative Porter Goss, FLORIDA

½ cup white flour, sifted
1½ cups whole wheat flour
½ teaspoon salt
1 tablespoon sugar
1 teaspoon baking soda
½ teaspoon cream of tartar
2 tablespoons shortening
¾ cup buttermilk

Mix dry ingredients with a fork. Add shortening and buttermilk. If too dry, add more buttermilk. Knead 10 times. Form a circular loaf.

Cut a deep 1-inch cross in the top.

Bake on a cookie sheet for 50 minutes at 375 degrees.

Makes wonderful toast.

PEACH MUFFINS

Senator Christopher Bond, MISSOURI

2   cups unsifted flour
1   tablespoon baking powder
1   egg
¼   cup oil
1   cup milk
⅔   cup sugar
½   teaspoon salt
¼   teaspoon cinnamon
1   teaspoon lemon juice
¼   teaspoon vanilla
1   cup fresh peaches, chopped

Preheat oven to 450 degrees. Sift flour and baking powder together. Beat egg and stir in oil, milk, sugar, salt, cinnamon, lemon juice, and vanilla. Add flour mixture and stir until blended. Do not over-mix. Gently fold in peaches. Fill greased muffin cups ⅔ full. Bake 20 minutes.

Note: A cup of drained canned peaches packed in light syrup or water may be substituted.

Makes 18 to 20 muffins.

BLUEBERRY MUFFINS

Senator Tom Daschle, SOUTH DAKOTA

1 egg
1 cup milk
¼ cup vegetable oil or butter
2 cups flour
¼ cup sugar
1 teaspoon baking powder
1 teaspoon salt
1 cup blueberries

Beat egg well. Add milk and oil or butter. Mix the dry ingredients in separate bowl and add liquids. Fold gently.

Add the blueberries and fill greased muffin cups ⅔ full.

Bake for 15 minutes at 400 degrees.

Makes 1 dozen muffins.

OATMEAL PANCAKES

Senator Chuck Grassley, IOWA

2	eggs
1½	cups buttermilk
1	cup oatmeal
1	teaspoon baking powder
1	teaspoon baking soda
½	teaspoon salt
1	teaspoon sugar
⅓	cup flour

Beat eggs.

Mix and let set a few minutes for oatmeal to soak up a bit of moisture. Cook in a hot skillet as you do other pancakes.

Makes 8 pancakes.

FAVORITE DINNER ROLLS

Representative Mike DeWine, OHIO

2 packages active dry yeast
½ cup warm water
½ cup margarine
1½ cups scalded milk, cooled to lukewarm
1 teaspoon salt
2 eggs
½ cup honey
7 to 7½ cups flour (part whole wheat if desired)
Butter

Dissolve yeast in warm water. Melt margarine in milk and combine with next 3 ingredients and 4 cups of flour. Beat until smooth. Mix in enough remaining flour to make dough easy to handle. Turn dough onto lightly floured surface; knead until smooth and elastic, about 3 to 5 minutes.

Place in greased bowl and grease top of dough. Cover and let rise in warm place until double—about 1½ to 2 hours. Punch dough down and divide into 4 parts. To make crescent rolls, roll dough into 12-inch flat circle, about ¼-inch thick. Spread with soft butter. Cut into 16 wedges. Roll up, beginning at rounded edge. Place rolls on baking sheet and curve slightly.

For Parkerhouse rolls, roll dough into 9- by 13-inch oblong pan about ½ inch thick. Cut into 3-inch circles. Put pat of butter in each circle and fold so top half overlaps slightly. Press edges together. Place on cookie sheets. Bake at 350 degrees for 15 to 25 minutes. Makes 4 dozen rolls. May be frozen.

MASSACHUSETTS CRANBERRY BREAD

★

Senator John Kerry, MASSACHUSETTS

¼ cup butter or margarine, softened

1 cup sugar

2 eggs

1 cup Massachusetts cranberries, chopped

½ cup water

½ teaspoon vanilla

1¾ cups flour

½ teaspoon baking soda

1½ teaspoons baking powder

1 teaspoon salt

½ teaspoon cinnamon

½ cup walnuts, chopped

Grease and flour a loaf pan. Cream the butter or margarine and sugar together in a large mixing bowl. Beat in the eggs with an electric mixer. Stir in cranberries, water, and vanilla. Sift the flour, baking soda, baking powder, salt, and cinnamon together and stir in with the butter. Add the chopped walnuts to the mixture and pour into the loaf pan.

Bake at 350 degrees for 55 minutes. Test with a toothpick for doneness.

DATE AND NUT BREAD

Representative Ron Paul, TEXAS

2   teaspoons baking soda
1   pound dates, chopped
1   pint boiling water
3   tablespoons butter
1½ cups sugar
2   eggs, beaten
½   teaspoon salt
3   cups flour
1   cup walnuts, chopped
1   tablespoon vanilla

Sprinkle baking soda over chopped dates. Pour in boiling water and stir. Add butter, sugar, and eggs to mixture. Add salt, flour, nuts, and vanilla. Pour batter into 4 greased 7½- by 3½- by 2-inch loaf pans.

Bake 45 minutes at 350 degrees or until toothpick comes out clean. Makes 4 medium-sized loaves. Only fifteen minutes preparation time and suitable for freezing.

AUNT DEDA'S
HOMEMADE BISCUITS

Representative Jerry Costello, ILLINOIS

2 cups Gold Medal self-rising flour
2 tablespoons Crisco shortening
3 tablespoons Crisco shortening, melted
  Buttermilk

Crumble flour and 2 tablespoons Crisco. Add buttermilk to moisten. Form into loose ball. Lay ball of dough on floured surface. Pat down gently with heavily floured hands. DO NOT ROLL OUT. Cut biscuits. Place in a greased 9- by 13-inch glass baking dish. Brush melted Crisco on top of biscuits. Bake at 400 degrees for 40 to 45 minutes. Brown, if necessary, using broiler for only a few seconds.

CAKES AND COOKIES

★ 9

MELT IN YOUR MOUTH BLUEBERRY CAKE

Senator Susan M. Collins, MAINE

    2   eggs, separated
    1   cup sugar
    ½   cup shortening
    ¼   teaspoon salt
    1   teaspoon vanilla
    1½ cups flour, sifted
    1   teaspoon baking powder
    ⅓   cup milk
    1½ cups fresh Maine blueberries

Beat egg whites until stiff in a small glass bowl. Add about ¼ cup of the sugar to keep them stiff. Cream shortening and add salt and vanilla. Add remaining sugar gradually. Add unbeaten egg yolks and beat until light and creamy.

Add dry ingredients alternately with milk. Fold in beaten whites. Fold in lightly floured fresh berries. Turn into greased 8- by 8-inch pan and sprinkle top with sugar.

Bake in a 350-degree oven for 50 to 60 minutes.

Makes 8 servings.

> This is a recipe that my mother has perfected over time.

CONGRESSMAN WAXMAN'S FAVORITE CAKE

★

Representative Henry Waxman, CALIFORNIA

2	cups apple slices, peeled and diced
½ to 1	cup sugar, depending on tartness of the apples
¾	cup safflower oil
1	beaten egg
1	cup flour
1	teaspoon cinnamon
¼	teaspoon salt
1	teaspoon vanilla
1	teaspoon baking soda
½	cup walnuts, chopped
½	cup currants, plumped in water
1	teaspoon grated orange rind to taste

Place apples and sugar in a bowl. Let stand 30 minutes or more. Add and mix oil, egg, flour, cinnamon, salt, vanilla, baking soda, walnuts, and currants. Mix well.

Bake in a well-greased 8-inch pan for about 45 minutes. Cool in pan for 10 minutes.

Serve with ice cream or whipped cream.

KAHLUA CHOCOLATE FUDGE CAKE

Senator Joe Biden, DELAWARE

PECAN PAN COATING:

1 tablespoon butter

¼ cup pecans, finely chopped

1 teaspoon sugar

CAKE:

¾ cup unsweetened cocoa

1 cup boiling water

½ cup Kahlua, divided

1⅔ cups flour, sifted

1 teaspoon baking soda

½ teaspoon baking powder

½ teaspoon salt

¾ cup butter

1½ cups sugar

3 large eggs, beaten

3 tablespoons raspberry jam

FROSTING:

6 ounces semisweet chocolate chips

½ cup butter

1 teaspoon instant coffee

¼ cup Kahlua

PECAN PAN COATING:

Butter sides of 9-inch springform pan. Spread butter in bottom of pan. Sprinkle with pecans and sugar. Set aside.

(Continued)

CAKE:

Mix cocoa with boiling water; let cool and then add ¼ cup Kahlua. Set aside. Mix flour, baking soda, baking powder, and salt together. Set aside. Cream butter and sugar until fluffy. Add beaten eggs. Blend dry ingredients into cream mixture alternately with cocoa mixture. Pour into springform pan. Bake at 325 degrees for 60 to 70 minutes. Cool in pan for 10 minutes only. Remove sides; let cool.

Pan coating will serve as bottom of cake. Cut cake in half horizontally. Drizzle remaining Kahlua over each half. Spread jam over bottom layer. Spread with ¼ cup of Kahlua frosting. Sandwich cake and frost all over.

FROSTING:

Melt semisweet morsels on top of double boiler. Gradually beat in butter and instant coffee granules dissolved in Kahlua. Beat until smooth.

Note: Cake should rest overnight.

JILL'S CHOCOLATE CAKE

Senator Joe Biden, DELAWARE

1   8-ounce package cream cheese, room temperature
2   1-pound boxes powdered sugar
1   teaspoon vanilla
½   cup butter, room temperature
5   squares unsweetened chocolate, melted
½   cup milk, room temperature
2½ cups flour
⅓   cup butter
4   eggs
1½ cups milk
    Dash of salt
1   teaspoon baking powder
1   teaspoon baking soda

Mix first 6 ingredients together. Divide this mixture in half. One half will be your icing.

To the other half add the remaining ingredients. Place in 2 round 9-inch baking pans, greased. Bake at 350 degrees for 30 to 40 minutes. Let cool and ice with other half of first mixture.

This is our family's favorite chocolate cake recipe.

LEMON JELLO CAKE

★

Senator Russ Feingold, WISCONSIN

1   small package lemon jelly powder

1   cup boiling water

¾   cup oil

1   package yellow cake mix

4   eggs

1   cup powdered sugar

1   large lemon, juiced

Dissolve package of lemon jelly powder in boiling water. Cool. Add oil to package of cake mix. Beat well.

Add eggs, one at a time. Beat well after each addition.

Add cooled lemon jelly. Beat very, very well. Pour into greased 9- by 13-inch pan. Bake at 350 degrees for 40 minutes.

While cake is still hot, prick cake all over with fork. Drizzle powdered sugar mixed with lemon juice over warm cake. Cut into squares to serve.

This recipe is from my mother, Sylvia Feingold. She has made it for years for many to enjoy.

FRUIT COCKTAIL CAKE

Senator Daniel Inouye, HAWAII

1   18½-ounce package banana cake mix
1   3¾-ounce package banana instant pudding mix
1   16-ounce can fruit cocktail, drained and syrup reserved
1   cup coconut, shredded
4   eggs, room temperature
¼   cup vegetable oil
½   cup brown sugar, firmly packed
½   cup macadamia nuts, chopped

GLAZE AND GARNISH:
½   cup butter
⅓   cup sugar
½   cup evaporated milk
1   teaspoon vanilla
1   cup coconut, shredded, for garnish

Mix together cake mix, pudding mix, fruit cocktail syrup, shredded coconut, eggs, and oil. Beat for 2 minutes. Fold in fruit cocktail. Pour into greased 9- by 13-inch pan or two 8- by 8-inch pans. Mix together brown sugar and nuts. Sprinkle over cake batter. Bake in preheated 325-degree oven for 45 minutes. Do not underbake. Cool for 15 minutes.

Meanwhile, prepare glaze by combining butter, sugar, evaporated milk, and vanilla in saucepan. Bring ingredients to a boil. Simmer for 2 minutes. Sprinkle coconut over cake while hot. Spoon hot glaze over coconut.

This is a variation of a recipe from Mrs. Thomas J. McCabe of Honolulu.

CARROT CAKE

Senator Carl Levin, MICHIGAN

1   cup flour
¾   cup sugar
1   teaspoon baking powder
¾   teaspoon baking soda
½   teaspoon ground cinnamon
½   teaspoon salt
2   eggs
¾   cup vegetable oil
1   cup carrots, grated
½   cup crushed pineapple, drained
½   cup walnuts, coarsely chopped

FROSTING:
6   tablespoons butter
1   3-ounce package cream cheese
½   teaspoon vanilla
3   heaping tablespoons confectioners' sugar

To prepare cake, put all dry ingredients in food processor bowl and mix 5 to 10 seconds. Add eggs and oil and mix 30 seconds; mixture will be very thick. Add carrots and pineapple and process thoroughly. Add nuts and process only to distribute. Bake in greased pan in preheated 350-degree oven about 1 hour.

To prepare frosting, process butter, cream cheese, and vanilla for about 20 seconds. Add sugar and continue mixing. When cake is cold, pat frosting all over.

This recipe is designed for a food processor; however, it can be adapted to a mixer.

WHIPPED CREAM POUND CAKE

Representative Trent Lott, MISSISSIPPI

  3   cups sugar
  1   cup butter, softened
  6   eggs, room temperature
  3   cups cake flour, sifted
  ½   pint whipping cream, whipped
  2   teaspoons vanilla

Cream sugar and butter. Add eggs one at a time and beat well after each one. Add flour and cream alternately. Add vanilla.

Pour in large greased and floured tube pan. Place in cold oven and bake at 325 degrees for 1 hour and 15 minutes.

Top with berries or powdered sugar or enjoy plain for a tasty treat.

DAISY'S WHITE CAKE

Representative Porter Goss, FLORIDA

1 cup butter

2 cups sugar

3 cups flour, sifted

2 teaspoons baking powder

1 cup milk

6 egg whites, beaten

ICING:

3 squares unsweetened chocolate

1 tablespoon butter

2 tablespoons cream

1 pound powdered sugar

Cream butter and sugar. Add flour, baking powder, and milk. Stir well. Gently fold in the egg whites last. Bake at 350 degrees for 30 minutes in 2 well-greased 9-inch pans.

For icing, melt first 3 ingredients. Beat in sifted powdered sugar until thick. Spread on cake when cool.

DOUBLE DIP CHOCOLATE CHIP COOKIES

Senator Christopher Bond, MISSOURI

4 cups semisweet chocolate chips
1 cup brown sugar
1 cup sugar
1 cup margarine
2 eggs
1 teaspoon vanilla
1 teaspoon baking soda
1 teaspoon salt
3 cups flour
1 cup pecans, chopped

Preheat oven to 375 degrees. Reserve 1½ cups of chocolate chips for dipping.

Cream sugars, margarine, eggs, and vanilla until light. Add baking soda, salt, and flour gradually, mixing until smooth. Add remaining chocolate chips and the pecans. Using a measuring teaspoon, drop rounded spoonfuls of dough about 3 inches apart on a foil-covered baking sheet, flattening each mound slightly with palm of hand. Bake 8 to 10 minutes or until done. Remove from baking sheet; cool on rack.

Melt reserved chocolate chips. Dip half of each cooled cookie in chocolate. Spread chocolate evenly over cookie half. If chocolate is too thick, remove excess with a knife. Place cookies on waxed paper. Cool in a refrigerator until chocolate hardens.

Makes 4 dozen.

Our son Samuel thinks the extra dip of chocolate makes this a stellar afternoon treat with a cold glass of milk.

GERMAN CHOCOLATE CARAMEL BARS

★

Senator Christopher Bond, MISSOURI

14 ounces caramels
5 ounces evaporated milk, divided
1 package German chocolate cake mix with pudding
½ cup margarine, melted
1 cup pecans, chopped
6 ounces chocolate chips

Preheat oven to 350 degrees. In a saucepan over low heat, melt caramels with ⅓ cup evaporated milk. Combine remaining milk with cake mix, margarine, and pecans. Batter will be stiff.

Press half of cake mixture into a 9- by 13-inch pan and bake for 6 minutes. Sprinkle chocolate chips over crust. Add caramel mixture and spread to edges. Top with remaining cake mixture. Bake 15 to 20 minutes. Cool on rack, then refrigerate. Cut into bars for serving.

Makes 4 dozen.

Grandmother Ida Doerr Bond is believed to be the source for this family favorite from Perryville.

GOOEY BUTTER
COFFEE CAKE

★

Senator Christopher Bond, MISSOURI

1   16-ounce box pound cake mix

4   eggs

½   cup butter, melted

16   ounces confectioners' sugar

1   8-ounce package cream cheese, softened

1½   teaspoons vanilla

Preheat oven to 350 degrees. Combine cake mix, two of the eggs, and butter. Pour into a well-greased 9- by 13-inch baking pan. Reserve 2 tablespoons of sugar. Combine cream cheese, vanilla, remaining eggs, and sugar. Mix well and spread over batter. Bake for 15 minutes.

Remove from oven; sprinkle reserved sugar on top. Return to oven and continue baking for 25 minutes. Cool on rack or serve warm.

Makes 10 to 12 servings.

Long a St. Louis favorite. We discovered this "goodie" at a campaign coffee in Florissant.

APPLE DAPPLE CAKE

Senator Christopher Bond, MISSOURI

3 eggs
1½ cups salad oil
2 cups sugar
3 cups flour
1 teaspoon salt
1 teaspoon baking soda
4 cups apples, chopped
1½ cups pecans, chopped
2 teaspoons vanilla

GLAZE:
1 cup brown sugar
¼ cup milk
½ cup margarine or butter

Preheat oven to 350 degrees. Mix eggs, oil, and sugar and blend well. Sift flour, salt, and baking soda together and add to egg mixture. Add apples, nuts, and vanilla. Pour batter into greased tube or Bundt pan. Bake for 1 hour.

Remove from oven. In a saucepan, combine brown sugar, milk, and margarine. Simmer 2½ minutes. While cake is still hot, pour glaze over cake in pan. Cool cake completely before removing from pan.

Makes 18 servings.

No trip to Pike County is complete without a visit to the Stark Apple Orchards in Louisiana. Governor and Mrs. Lloyd Stark were longtime family friends. During the restoration of the Governor's Mansion, Mrs. Stark could not have been more helpful or supportive.

RHUBARB CAKE

Senator Chuck Grassley, IOWA

1	cup sugar
1	cup sour cream
1	egg
1½	cups flour
1	teaspoon baking soda
½	teaspoon salt
3	cups freshly cut rhubarb, chopped
1	teaspoon vanilla
1	cup brown sugar
1	teaspoon cinnamon

Using a mixer, beat together the sugar, sour cream, and egg. Add the flour, baking soda, and salt. Stir in the rhubarb by hand.

Pour in greased 9- by 13-inch pan. Top with mixture of vanilla, brown sugar, and cinnamon.

Bake at 375 degrees for 40 to 45 minutes.

From Esther, who has given my wife many great recipes.

CURRENT RIVER CHOCOLATE SHEET CAKE

Senator Christopher Bond, MISSOURI

1 cup butter

½ cup cocoa

1 cup water

2 cups sugar

2 cups flour, unsifted

1 teaspoon baking soda

2 eggs, slightly beaten

½ cup sour cream

2 teaspoons vanilla

Always tucked away in a cooler for our float trips on the Current River, this delicious yet easy dessert is the first to disappear at a carry-in supper.

CHOCOLATE NUT ICING:

½ cup butter

¼ cup cocoa

6 tablespoons evaporated milk

16 ounces confectioners' sugar

1 cup walnuts, chopped

1 teaspoon vanilla

Preheat oven to 350 degrees. Thoroughly grease a 15½- by 10½-inch jelly roll pan. Combine butter, cocoa, and water in a saucepan and bring to a fell boil. While still hot, pour mixture over combined sugar, flour, and baking soda. Mix well. Add eggs, sour cream, and vanilla. Mix well. Pour batter into pan, bake 15 minutes. Do not overbake.

While cake is baking, make the icing. Mix butter, cocoa, and milk in a saucepan; heat to boiling point. Add confectioners' sugar, walnuts, and vanilla and mix well. Additional milk may be added to make icing more spreadable. Ice cake immediately after removing from oven.

Makes 20 to 24 servings.

COCOA CAKE

Senator Chuck Grassley, IOWA

1½ cups sugar
½ cup shortening
½ teaspoon salt
2 eggs
¾ cup sour milk or buttermilk
1 teaspoon baking soda
1½ cups flour
3 heaping tablespoons cocoa
1 teaspoon vanilla
½ cup boiling water

Cream the sugar, shortening, and salt. Add eggs and beat. Mix buttermilk and baking soda and add to creamed mixture, alternately with flour and cocoa. Add vanilla. Last, add boiling water. Pour batter into greased 9- by 13-inch pan. Bake for 35 minutes at 350 degrees.

This is one of my mother-in-law's favorite standbys. My wife has been making it since she was in high school.

DEEP SOUTH
SYRUP CAKE

Senator John Breaux, LOUISIANA

½ cup vegetable oil

1½ cups cane syrup

1 egg, well beaten

2½ cups flour, sifted

1 teaspoon ground ginger

½ teaspoon salt (optional)

1½ teaspoons baking soda

¾ cup hot water

½ cup pecans, chopped, or raisins

Grease and flour a 9- by 13-inch pan. Preheat oven to 350 degrees.

Combine oil, syrup, and beaten egg and stir until well blended. Mix dry ingredients except baking soda. Mix soda and hot water, then add to syrup mixture. Combine syrup mixture and flour mixture; stir until well blended.

Add pecans or raisins at this time and blend. Pour into prepared pan and bake for 45 minutes. Cut into squares and serve with Cool Whip.

POUND CAKE

Senator Robert Byrd, WEST VIRGINIA

2   cups sugar

1   cup white vegetable shortening

3   cups flour

½   teaspoon baking powder

½   teaspoon baking soda

4   eggs

1   teaspoon vanilla or almond extract

1   cup buttermilk

Cream sugar and shortening. Sift dry ingredients together and add eggs, flavoring, and half the milk. Beat 2 minutes and add remaining milk. Beat 2 more minutes.

Bake in 2 greased, waxed paper–lined 8- by 3-inch loaf pans at 325 degree for 45 to 50 minutes.

Makes 2 cake loaves.

WORLD SERIES BROWNIES

Senator Christopher Bond, MISSOURI

2   cups butter
8   squares unsweetened chocolate
8   eggs
4   cups sugar
    Pinch of salt
1   teaspoon vanilla
2   cups flour, sifted
2   cups walnuts, chopped

ICING:

⅓   cup cocoa
⅓   cup butter
¼   cup milk
1   cup confectioners' sugar
1   teaspoon vanilla

Preheat oven to 350 degrees. Melt butter and chocolate over hot water in double boiler and set aside to cool. Beat eggs and add sugar, salt, and vanilla. Add cooled chocolate mixture. Fold in flour and chopped nuts. Pour into greased and floured 9- by 13-inch pan. Bake at 350 degrees for 45 to 60 minutes over pan of hot water.

Combine all icing ingredients, except vanilla, and boil 3 minutes. Add vanilla and beat a few minutes. Pour icing over brownies. Cool and cut into 1½-inch squares.

Makes 6 dozen.

This was named because my wife packed a container of these before we boarded a Governor's World Series Whistle-Stop Train across Missouri on October 21, 1985. A friend from Greene County gets the credit for the brownie recipe.

SPICY APPLE COOKIES

Senator Chuck Grassley, IOWA

½ cup shortening
1½ cups brown sugar
1 egg
2 cups flour
½ teaspoon cinnamon
¼ teaspoon nutmeg
½ teaspoon baking powder
½ teaspoon cloves
½ teaspoon baking soda
¼ cup milk
1 cup apple, grated
1 cup raisins
½ cup walnuts

Cream shortening, sugar, and egg. Sift dry ingredients and add alternately with milk. Add apple, raisins, and nuts.

Bake on shallow baking sheet at 350 degrees until done. Ice with your favorite vanilla frosting while hot.

RED VELVET CAKE

Representative Nick Lampson, TEXAS

½ cup shortening
1½ cups sugar
2 eggs
2½ cups flour
1 teaspoon cocoa
½ teaspoon salt
1 tablespoon vanilla
1 cup buttermilk
2 ounces red food coloring
1 teaspoon baking soda
1 teaspoon vinegar

ICING:
1 cup milk
¼ cup flour
½ cup shortening
1 stick margarine
1 cup powdered sugar
1 teaspoon vanilla
Dash of salt

Preheat oven to 350 degrees. Grease and flour two 9-inch cake pans. Cream shortening, sugar, and eggs. Add flour, cocoa, salt, vanilla, and buttermilk. Fold in red food coloring, baking soda, and vinegar. Bake 30 to 35 minutes.

For icing, cook milk and flour over low heat to pudding stage. Place in refrigerator until cool.

In a separate bowl, cream shortening, margarine, powdered sugar, vanilla, and salt. Add to pudding mixture and beat until smooth. Spread on cake.

SENATOR JOHN WARNER'S FAVORITE COOKIES

★

Senator John Warner, VIRGINIA

½ pound butter

¾ cup sugar

1 cup brown sugar

2 eggs

1 teaspoon vanilla

1½ cups flour

1 teaspoon baking soda

1 cup coconut, flaked

1½ cups semisweet chocolate chips

¼ cup dates, chopped

½ cup sunflower seeds

¼ cup almonds, chopped

Cream the butter and add sugars, eggs, and vanilla. Stir in the flour and baking soda. Add the remaining ingredients.

Drop spoonful sizes of dough onto baking sheets. Bake at 325 degrees for 12 minutes.

Makes 2 to 3 dozen cookies.

KAY'S COOKIES

Representative Kay Granger, TEXAS

2 cups flour

1 teaspoon baking soda

½ teaspoon salt

½ teaspoon baking powder

1¼ cups shortening (butter flavored adds flavor)

¾ cup sugar

¾ cup brown sugar, packed

2 eggs, well beaten

1 teaspoon vanilla

2 cups coconut, shredded

2 cups Corn Flakes

1 cup pecans, chopped

Sift together flour, baking soda, salt, and baking powder. In a large mixing bowl, cream together the shortening and sugars until light and fluffy. Add eggs and vanilla.

Add sifted ingredients to the creamed mixture. Mix well for 2 minutes on medium speed. Fold in coconut, Corn Flakes, and pecans. Drop by the teaspoonful on ungreased cookie sheets.

Bake at 350 degrees for 8 minutes or until lightly browned. Cool on baking racks and then transfer to container.

Kay's cookies are made from a favorite family recipe. The Grangers and O'Days (Kay's sister Lynn and her family) have been enjoying these cookies for many, many years.

COWBOY COOKIES

President and Mrs. George W. Bush

1½ cups butter
1½ cups sugar
1½ cups brown sugar
 3 eggs
 1 tablespoon vanilla
 3 cups flour
 1 tablespoon baking powder
 1 tablespoon baking soda
 1 teaspoon salt
 1 tablespoon cinnamon
 3 cups chocolate chips
 3 cups oats
 2 cups coconut
 2 cups pecans

Cream butter and sugars. Add eggs and vanilla. Beat. Add dry ingredients until blended. Stir in remaining ingredients. Bake at 350 degrees for 10 to 12 minutes.

FAVORITE COCONUT CAKE

★

Representative Albert R. Wynn, MARYLAND

2 cups flour
1 tablespoon baking powder
1 cup butter
2 cups sugar
5 eggs
1 teaspoon coconut extract
1 cup buttermilk
1 cup coconut, flaked

Preheat oven to 350 degrees. Grease and flour 9- by 13-inch pan. Mix flour and baking powder together then set aside. In a large bowl, cream butter and sugar until light and fluffy.

Add eggs and beat well. Mix in coconut flavoring. Add flour mixture alternately with buttermilk, mixing well with each addition. Fold in coconut flakes. Pour batter into prepared pan.

Bake at 350 degrees for 1 hour or until a toothpick inserted into the cake comes out clean.

SPECIAL K BARS

Senator Byron Dorgan, NORTH DAKOTA

> 1 cup sugar
> 1 cup light corn syrup
> ¾ cup smooth or crunchy peanut butter
> 5 to 6 cups Special K cereal
> 6 ounces butterscotch chips
> 6 ounces chocolate chips

Heat sugar and syrup on stove, stirring until mixture comes to a boil. Remove from stove and add peanut butter and Special K. Press mixture in a greased 8- by 8-inch pan. Melt butterscotch and chocolate chips together. Spread over ingredients in pan. Cut into bars and serve.

DOUBLE CHOCOLATE BISCOTTI

★

Senator John Sununu, NEW HAMPSHIRE

⅓ cup butter, room temperature

⅔ cup sugar

¼ cup unsweetened cocoa

2 teaspoons baking powder

2 eggs

1¾ cups flour

4 ounces white chocolate, coarsely chopped

6 ounces semisweet chocolate chips

In a large bowl, beat butter until light. Add sugar, cocoa, and baking powder. Beat until fluffy. Mix in eggs. Mix in as much of the flour as you can. Stir in the remaining flour by hand. Add the white chocolate and semisweet chocolate chips. Divide dough in half. Shape each portion into a 9-inch roll. Place both on a greased cookie sheet 4 inches apart. Flatten each roll until 2 inches wide. Bake at 375 degrees for 20 to 25 minutes or until fairly firm to the touch. Cool slightly. With serrated knife, cut each roll into ½-inch diagonal slices. Lay slices, cut side down, on baking sheet. Bake at 325 degrees for 8 minutes. Turn slices over and bake for 8 minutes more until biscotti are dry and crisp.

Preparation time is 50 minutes. Suitable for freezing.

MACADAMIA DELIGHTS

Senator James M. Talent, MISSOURI

- 2 cups flour
- ½ teaspoon baking soda
- ¼ teaspoon salt
- ¾ cup unsalted butter, slightly softened
- ½ cup sugar
- ¾ cup dark brown sugar, firmly packed
- 2 eggs
- 2 teaspoons vanilla
- 1 cup sweetened coconut, shredded
- 1 cup macadamia nuts, coarsely chopped
- 12 ounces white chocolate, broken into chunks

Preheat oven to 300 degrees. Combine flour, baking soda, and salt in a bowl. Mix well. In a large bowl, mix the butter and sugars until coarsely blended. Add the eggs and vanilla; blend until smooth. Gradually add the flour mixture and blend until smooth. Add the coconut and mix thoroughly.

Add the macadamia nuts and white chocolate to the blended dough. Use a large spoon to fold these ingredients into the dough. To form the cookies, take about a tablespoon of dough and roll it into a ball.

Place the balls on an ungreased cookie sheet and freeze for about 5 to 10 minutes to harden the cookie dough.

Place the cookie sheet in the oven and bake for 18 to 23 minutes. The cookies should be a light brown when done.

Makes 4 to 5 dozen cookies. Suitable for freezing.

DOUBLE COCONUT MACAROONS

Senator Norm Coleman, MINNESOTA

14 ounces coconut, flaked, divided

⅔ cup powdered sugar, packed

¼ cup cream of coconut (Coco Lopez)

1 ounce cream cheese, softened

3 tablespoons flour

1 large egg white

½ teaspoon vanilla

Pinch of salt

1 pound bittersweet chocolate

Preheat oven to 325 degrees. Line large, heavy baking sheet with parchment paper or heavy-duty foil. Butter paper lightly or butter and flour lightly. Shake off excess flour.

Using food processor, chop 7 ounces of coconut and powdered sugar until mixture is moist. Add cream of coconut, cream cheese, flour, egg white, vanilla, and salt. Process until well blended, scraping down sides of bowl. Place remaining coconut in pie plate. Drop rounded tablespoons of dough into coconut and roll to coat completely. Using palms of hands, gently roll into balls with a 1½-inch diameter.

Bake macaroons until golden brown and just firm to the touch for 35 minutes. Cool completely on rack.

Melt bittersweet chocolate—do not overheat. Use double boiler over low heat. I usually heat water and place chocolate in top of double boiler or in bowl and then remove from heat and let melt slowly.

Dip bottom of each macaroon into chocolate; scrape off excess chocolate by wiping macaroon on rim of double boiler. Place on sheet lined with waxed paper and refrigerate until chocolate sets.

Macaroons may be prepared ahead. Store in airtight container and refrigerate up to 3 days or freeze for up to 3 weeks. Bring to room temperature before serving.

KENTUCKY JAM CAKE

Representative Ron Lewis, KENTUCKY

CAKE:

- 1¾ cups flour
- 1½ cups sugar
- 1 cup salad oil
- 3 eggs
- 1 cup buttermilk
- 1 cup blackberry jam
- 1 teaspoon baking soda
- 1 teaspoon baking powder
- 1 cup walnuts, chopped

CARAMEL FROSTING:

- ½ cup butter
- 1 cup confectioners' sugar
- 1½ cups brown sugar
- 1 teaspoon cinnamon
- 1 teaspoon nutmeg
- 1 teaspoon allspice
- 1 teaspoon vanilla
- ½ teaspoon cloves
- ½ teaspoon salt

Mix all cake ingredients together and beat. Grease and flour two 9-inch pans. Fill pans with cake batter and bake 30 to 35 minutes at 350 degrees. Ice with caramel frosting.

For frosting, combine first 3 ingredients. Bring to a boil for 2 minutes. Sift confectioners' sugar and beat into mixture. Add more sugar if needed.

Hint: For best results, an apple cut in half and placed in the cake box will keep the cake fresh several days longer. Suitable for freezing.

RAISIN CAKE
(DEPRESSION CAKE)

Representative Frank Pallone, NEW JERSEY

2 cups sugar

1 cup butter or margarine

½ teaspoon salt

2 teaspoons cinnamon

1 teaspoon cloves

¼ teaspoon nutmeg

1½ cups raisins

2 cups strong coffee

2 teaspoons baking soda dissolved in ¼ cup hot water

4 cups flour

In a large pot, mix sugar, butter, salt, spices, and raisins. Pour in strong coffee (you may use instant). Bring mixture to a boil. Continue to boil for 5 minutes. Cool completely and add baking soda and water mixture. Add flour, 1 cup at a time. Mix well. Pour into large 9- by 13-inch pan and bake at 350 degrees for 45 minutes.

TEXAS SWEETIES

Representative Ron Paul, TEXAS

COOKIES:

    1   cup butter or margarine, softened
    2   cups sugar
    3   eggs, beaten
    1   tablespoon almond extract
    3½ cups flour
    1   tablespoon baking powder
    ½   teaspoon salt

GLAZE:

    Confectioners' sugar
    Milk
    Almond extract

Cream butter and sugar. Add eggs and extract. Mix and add remaining ingredients. Form dough into 1½-inch balls and place on greased cookie sheet. Bake at 375 degrees for 10 to 12 minutes.

Combine ingredients for glaze. Glaze cookies when cool.

Makes 3 dozen.

NUTTY FINGER COOKIES

Senator Elizabeth Dole, NORTH CAROLINA

1   cup butter
4   tablespoons confectioners' sugar
2   cups pecans, broken
2   cups flour
1   teaspoon water
1   teaspoon vanilla
    Confectioners' sugar for dusting

Mix first 6 ingredients together. Flour hands and roll by the teaspoonful into shape of a date. Place on greased cookie sheet and crease top lengthwise with a knife. Bake at 250 to 300 degrees for 1 hour. Roll in confectioners' sugar while still warm.

Makes 50 cookies.

OATMEAL CHOCOLATE CHIP COOKIES

Senator Hillary Rodham Clinton, NEW YORK

1½ cups flour
1 teaspoon salt
1 teaspoon baking soda
1 cup shortening
½ cup sugar
1 cup brown sugar, packed
1 teaspoon vanilla
2 eggs
2 cups rolled oats
2 cups semisweet chocolate chips

Preheat oven to 350 degrees. Brush baking sheets lightly with vegetable oil. Combine flour, salt, and baking soda. In large bowl of electric mixer, beat together shortening, sugars, vanilla, and eggs until creamy.

Gradually beat in flour mixture. Stir in rolled oats and then chocolate chips. Drop batter by the rounded teaspoonful onto baking sheets. Bake for 8 to 10 minutes or until golden. Cool cookies on sheets for 2 minutes. Remove to wire racks to cool completely.

Makes 3 dozen.

PIES AND
DESSERTS

★ 10

Pies,
Mousses,
and Puddings

SOUTH ALABAMA PEANUT CLUSTERS

Senator Jeff Sessions, ALABAMA

    2   cups chocolate almond bark
    1   cup smooth peanut butter
    3   cups miniature marshmallows
    3   cups Rice Krispies
    2   cups dry roasted peanuts

Place almond bark in a 3-quart microwavable dish. Heat on full power 3 to 5 minutes or until melted. Stir often. Blend in peanut butter. Put dry ingredients in a large bowl and pour hot mixture over them.

Blend well. Drop by teaspoonful onto waxed paper.

Makes a lot!

BISCOCHITOS

★

Representative Tom Udall, NEW MEXICO

2 cups lard

1 cup sugar

1 teaspoon anise seed

2 egg yolks

6 cups flour, sifted

3 teaspoons baking powder

1 teaspoon salt

½ cup orange juice

2 teaspoons cinnamon

½ cup sugar

Cream lard and sugar; add anise seed and beaten egg yolks. Sift flour, baking powder, and salt together. Alternately add flour and orange juice to first mixture.

Knead well until mixed. Roll out ⅛-inch thick and cut with your favorite holiday cutter or fancy shapes.

Combine cinnamon and sugar and sprinkle over cookies. Bake in moderate oven for 8 to 10 minutes until golden brown.

A popular holiday favorite in New Mexico, these tasty treats are splendid.

PECAN PRALINES

★

Senator John Breaux, LOUISIANA

  1   cup sugar
  2   cups brown sugar
  ¾   cup condensed milk (not evaporated)
  ½   cup water
  2   teaspoons white corn syrup
      Pinch of baking soda
 15   large marshmallows
  4   cups small to medium pecan halves

Mix all ingredients except marshmallows and pecans. Bring to a boil and cook until soft-ball stage (235 degrees), stirring constantly.

Remove from heat and add marshmallows. Return to heat and cook until soft-ball stage again.

Remove from heat, add pecans, and beat until mixture thickens. Spoon out quickly onto waxed paper and let set until firm.

Makes 36 pralines.

MOM'S ENGLISH SCONES

★

Senator James Inhofe, OKLAHOMA

 2   cups flour
 ¼   cup sugar
 ½   teaspoon salt
 2½ teaspoons baking powder
 ½   teaspoon baking soda
 ¼   cup shortening
 ¼   cup currants
 1   cup buttermilk

Sift dry ingredients and cut into shortening. Add currants and buttermilk (dough will be sticky). Knead 1 minute on floured surface and cut into rounds. Place on ungreased cookie sheet. Bake at 450 degrees for 12 to 15 minutes.

They are delicious while hot topped with whipped butter!

CHOCOLATE MOUSSE

Representative Ben Cardin, MARYLAND

2 4-ounce bars of German sweet chocolate
  Boiling water
6 eggs, separated
½ pint whipping cream
¼ tablespoon sugar

Break up chocolate bars. Place in large bowl. Add boiling water to cover chocolate and place dish towel on top of bowl. Let stand 5 minutes.

Whip egg whites until stiff but not dry. Whip cream.

Pour off water. Chocolate should be melted. Add egg yolks and sugar and mix well. Fold in whipped cream, then fold in stiff egg whites.

Pour mousse into bowl. Refrigerate at least 8 hours.

Serves 8.

For a change: Layer the mousse with open lady fingers, placing lady fingers on the bottom and ending with mousse on top.

Note: Save some of the whipped cream to decorate top of mousse.

APPLE CRUMBLE

Senator Paul Sarbanes, MARYLAND

1½	pounds large cooking apples
3 to 4	tablespoons sugar
½	lemon, juiced
¼	teaspoon cinnamon
¼	pound butter
2	cups flour
½	cup sugar
¼	teaspoon ground ginger

Peel, core, and slice apples. Mix in a 1-quart glass baking dish with sugar, lemon juice, and cinnamon.

Rub the butter into the flour until it is the consistency of fine bread crumbs. Add sugar and ground ginger and mix in well. Sprinkle the crumble over the apples and press down lightly.

Bake in a 350 degree oven for 30 to 40 minutes until golden brown and apples are cooked. Serve with a small jug of thick cream (unwhipped).

This is also good made with other fruit such as blueberries or peaches.

This is our family's favorite dessert and comes from England.

CONGRESSMAN PETER KING'S LEMON SQUARES

Representative Peter King, NEW YORK

1	cup butter
½	cup confectioners' sugar
2	cups flour
4	eggs
1½	cups sugar
4	tablespoons lemon juice
4	tablespoons flour

In a 9- by 12-inch baking pan, rub together butter, confectioners' sugar, and flour to make crumbles.

Bake in a 350 degree oven until the edges are golden brown.

Mix remaining ingredients together. Pour mixture over the baked crumbs and return the pan to the 350 degree oven.

Bake for about 10 to 15 minutes or until the lemon mixture is just about set. (You want the lemon mixture to be a little soft and wiggly.) Cool in the pan.

Sprinkle with confectioners' sugar and cut into squares.

Enjoy!

OKLAHOMA MUD

Representative J. C. Watts, OKLAHOMA

2 cups sugar
2 sticks of margarine, melted
4 eggs
1 teaspoon vanilla
1½ cups flour
1½ cups coconut
1½ cups nuts, chopped (pecans are great)
3 tablespoons cocoa
1 jar marshmallow cream

ICING:
1 box powdered sugar
1 stick margarine, melted
½ cup cocoa
½ cup evaporated milk
1 tablespoon vanilla

Cream sugar, margarine, eggs, and vanilla.

Mix together dry ingredients and fold into the creamed mixture. Spread into a greased and floured 9- by 13-inch pan and bake at 350 degrees for 45 minutes or until done.

After removing from oven, immediately spread marshmallow cream over the top.

While cake cools, combine ingredients for icing. Mix well and spread over the cooled cake.

I am proud to be a Congressman from the Fourth District of Oklahoma. But nothing thrills me more than being called Dad or a youth minister. It was such a privilege to be an influence on young lives and help steer and guide them through the tumultuous teen years. Cultural renewal in this country requires that the strong institutions like church, family, community, and schools be strengthened, and I got a firsthand lesson on that topic as a youth minister. This particular recipe came in handy with all of our church functions. It serves a bunch of hungry kids. We served this at a lot of church suppers when I was a youth minister.

JANE SPRATT'S DELUXE PECAN PIE

★

Representative John Spratt, SOUTH CAROLINA

⅔ cup brown sugar

⅓ cup white corn syrup

2 tablespoons milk

1 heaping tablespoon cornmeal

2 eggs, lightly beaten

Dash of salt

2 tablespoons butter, melted

1 cup pecan pieces

1 teaspoon vanilla

2 8-inch pie shells

Preheat oven to 375 degrees.

Mix ingredients in order listed.

Pour into pie shells. Bake for 25 minutes.

Makes 8 to 10 servings.

Here's one of my favorites, and a southern favorite as well.
—John Spratt

BLITZ KUCHEN

Senator George Voinovich, OHIO

3 eggs, separated
2 tablespoons butter
1¼ cups sugar
2 cups flour, sifted
Dash of salt
2 teaspoons baking powder
¾ cup milk
Rind and juice of lemon
2 teaspoons cinnamon
½ cup sugar

Cream egg yolks, butter, and sugar until light and creamy. Sift and measure flour; add salt and baking powder. Alternately add milk and flour mixture to batter. Beat until smooth. Add rind and juice of lemon.

Beat egg whites until stiff but not dry. Fold in carefully. Pour in a 9- by 13-inch oblong baking pan. Bake 25 to 30 minutes at 350 degrees. Sprinkle with cinnamon sugar mixture.

First made by Jan's mom in 1917!

ZOE'S PECAN PIE

Representative Zoe Lofgren, CALIFORNIA

CRUST:
- 1 cup flour
- Pinch of salt
- Generous ⅓ cup shortening
- 3 tablespoons cold water

FILLING:
- 3 eggs
- ½ cup sugar
- ⅓ cup dark corn syrup
- 1½ teaspoons vanilla
- Pinch of salt
- 1¼ cup pecan pieces

Mix flour and salt. Mix in shortening until crumbly. Avoid over-mixing when adding water. Press into an 8-inch pie pan.

Beat eggs well, then add the rest of the ingredients except for the pecans. Beat mixture well and pour into pie crust.

Add pecans to the mixture in the pan and stir, being careful not to puncture pie crust. Place pie in 350-degree oven and bake for 50 to 60 minutes or until done.

Enjoy!

HUCKLEBERRY PIE

Senator Max Baucus, MONTANA

½ cup sugar or honey
1   pint fresh huckleberries
1   tablespoon flour
1   9-inch unbaked pie shell
2   tablespoons butter

Mix sugar, huckleberries, and flour together. Place in pie shell and dot liberally with butter. Bake for 30 to 40 minutes at 350 degrees.

The "secret" of this recipe is the special berries that can only come from the mountainous elevations, chiefly in the west. The taste comes with the eating, but even more so if the person who makes the pie was in on the collection of the berries. They grow with abandon on green wooded slopes just under the treeline and may be accessible only by dirt roads (put there by timber companies of the U.S. Forest Service), preferably on sunny days in late July and early August. The choice spots vary each year, which means that pickers have elaborate games in store either to include or exclude fellow pickers from their favorite slopes.

Some people who would entertain a crowd with the results of the day's foray would never dream of revealing the lush and abundant grounds they trod in pursuit of their elusive prize. For these berries—which New Englanders are apt to call blueberries, although the two species do not taste the same to all connoisseurs—are shamelessly shy and do not readily reveal themselves to heavy-footed and acquisitive souls. They require some shade and moisture, and intermittent sun, before they develop their large, smooth, glistening roundness. So splendid and rare a taste they are that black, brown, even grizzly bears also treasure them and a person may run interference with one or more of these massive creatures when the season is at its height. The higher the elevation, the more likely the bears. So the picker dresses wisely, and watches well. He or she may add a tiny bell to the picking can (plastic buckets are best, with large handles) and so warn off the competitors. The bears need to fill up their stomachs in preparation for the long winter's hibernation ahead. The anxious pie lover (or jelly or jam maker, or syrup lover, or any of a number of combinations of these types) only stalks the lonely forests at this peril; but that also gives some added piquancy to the chase. Picking is handwork, unless you fall into the school that appreciates modern marvels and may then choose a carefully crafted wooden box with a claw-like aperture that can swoop through the berry bushes and haphazardly collect bunches that fall back into the receptacle below. But you are apt to collect just as many of the bitter green leaves as well.

Wardrobe is important, too, and the company one chooses. Always include a foul-weather slicker, in a bright color (those bears again—they are shy, too, and might back off if a yellow or red human being is on the trail), and a rain hat and heavy boots for climbing. Part of the fun is hiking with friends, picnicking in a lovely glen. Part of it is exercise—stopping constantly, and talking or singing as you go. The rest of the fun is filling the buckets and then dumping each one into the larger group pot at some central location, then, at the end of the afternoon, carrying home the precious and painfully acquired berries to be divided up among all—and eventually into pies. Best of all is baking one immediately, for a sort of instant reward, although the berries can be put into tiny plastic bags and stored in the refrigerator, even the freezer. (They can be a very liquid mass after thawing.)

This guarantees that a good pie is a good memory, and not just another meal.

LEMONADE PIE

★

Senator Chuck Grassley, IOWA

1   6-ounce can frozen lemonade
1   14-ounce can sweetened condensed milk
4   ounces Cool Whip
1   9-inch graham cracker crust

Thaw lemonade. Mix lemonade and milk. Fold into Cool Whip. Place in graham cracker crust. Chill. If desired, top with cherry or blueberry pie filling.

Guaranteed to get 'em home for dinner—even a Congressman!

SWISH PIE

★

Senator Chuck Grassley, IOWA

1	14-ounce can sweetened condensed milk
¼	cup lemon juice
½	cup walnuts, chopped
1	20-ounce can crushed pineapple, with juice
1	8-ounce tub Cool Whip
1	9-inch graham cracker crust

Mix milk and lemon juice. Add all other ingredients and place in graham cracker crust. Chill. Garnish with lemon slices or reserved pineapple or nuts.

Makes 2 pies.

This is oh, so good.

CAROL'S BUTTER CRUST

★

Senator Chuck Grassley, IOWA

½ cup butter, melted
1 cup flour
1 tablespoon sugar

Mix ingredients together in pie plate. Press out. Bake until brown, 10 to 12 minutes at 350 degrees.

Senator Christopher Bond, MISSOURI

GRAHAM CRACKER CRUST:
- 2⅓ cups cinnamon graham cracker crumbs
- ¾ cup butter, melted
- ⅓ cup sugar
- ⅔ cup cocoa, sifted

ICE CREAM FILLING:
- 2¾ pints vanilla ice cream
- ½ cup peanut butter
- ½ cup semisweet chocolate chips

CHOCOLATE SAUCE:
- 2 ounces unsweetened chocolate
- 3 tablespoons butter
- 1 cup sugar
- 1 rounded tablespoon flour
- 1 cup cold water
- 1 teaspoon vanilla

Mix together crumbs, butter, sugar, and cocoa until well combined. Press firmly into a 10-inch pie plate to make solid bottom. Freeze until ready to use.

By hand, combine ice cream with peanut butter and chocolate chips. Spoon into crust. Freeze immediately until solid, about 2 hours or overnight. Top each serving with chocolate sauce

Note: Do not let ice cream get too soft before mixing with peanut butter.

Top each serving with chocolate sauce.

(Continued)

In saucepan, melt chocolate and butter over low heat. Mix sugar and flour; add to chocolate mixture. Add water. Cook over medium heat, stirring constantly until thick. Add vanilla and beat until smooth.

Makes 8 servings.

Note: Do not let ice cream get too soft before mixing with peanut butter.

Guaranteed to be a hit with the preschool set and their parents. Combining all Sam's favorite things, this frozen delight is not for weight watchers.

CHIPPED CHOCOLATE PIE

Senator Orrin G. Hatch, UTAH

35 large marshmallows
½ cup milk
2 squares bitter or unsweetened chocolate, chipped
½ pint whipping cream, whipped, or 1 small container
    Cool Whip
1 10-inch graham cracker crust
    Chopped nuts, cherries, or chipped sweetened chocolate

Melt marshmallows with milk in double boiler or microwave. Cool. Beat well. Fold in bitter or unsweetened chocolate and whipped whipping cream. Pour into graham cracker crust. Top with chopped nuts, cherries, or chipped chocolate, as desired. Chill in refrigerator for at least 2 hours.

PUMPKIN TORTE

Senator Chuck Grassley, IOWA

CRUST:

  24 graham crackers, crushed

  ⅓ cup sugar

  ½ cup butter

FIRST LAYER:

  2 eggs, beaten

  ¾ cup sugar

  1 8-ounce package cream cheese

SECOND LAYER:

  2 cups pumpkin

  3 egg yolks

  ½ cup sugar

  ½ cup milk

  ½ teaspoon salt

  1 tablespoon cinnamon

  1 envelope gelatin

  ¼ cup cold water

  3 egg whites

  ¼ cup sugar

> Clipped from a farm magazine, and it's delicious. One of my favorites.

Mix crust ingredients and press into 9- by 13-inch pan. Mix first layer and pour over crust. Bake for 20 minutes at 350 degrees. Cool.

Meanwhile, cook pumpkin, egg yolks, sugar, milk, salt, and cinnamon until mixture thickens. Remove from heat. Dissolve gelatin in cold water and add to pumpkin mixture. Cool. Beat egg whites and sugar, then fold into cooled pumpkin mixture. Pour over cooled, baked crust. Refrigerate and serve with whipped cream.

BAKLAVA

Senator Olympia Snowe, MAINE

   1   pound butter
   1   pound phyllo dough (strudel leaves)
1½   pounds walnuts, chopped
 ¾   cup sugar
   1   teaspoon cinnamon
       Grated rind of 1 orange

SYRUP:
   2   cups water
   2   cups sugar
 ½   cup honey
   1   cinnamon stick
   3   lemon slices

Melt butter and brush on a 9- by 13-inch pan. Place 1 layer of phyllo in pan, allowing ends to extend over pan. Brush with melted butter. Repeat with 4 sheets of phyllo.

Mix nuts, sugar, cinnamon, and orange rind. Sprinkle phyllo heavily with nut mixture. Continue to alternate 1 layer of phyllo, brush with melted butter, then sprinkle heavily with nut mixture until all ingredients are used. Be sure to reserve 4 sheets of phyllo for the top (each to be brushed with butter).

Brush top with remaining butter, trim edges with sharp knife. Cut through top with diagonal lines to form diamond shapes. Bake at 400 degrees for 15 minutes. Lower oven to 300 degrees and continue to bake for 40 minutes. Should be golden brown in color.

To make syrup, cook first 4 ingredients over medium heat on stove until thick. Add lemon slices. Cook 3 minutes. Remove cinnamon and lemon.

(Continued)

While pastry is still hot, cover with prepared syrup and let stand overnight before serving. Baklava should rest for 24 hours before removing from pan. Will keep in refrigerator for weeks or can be frozen.

Makes 24 servings.

A Greek dessert, baklava was introduced to Greece in the sixth century by its Byzantine rulers, Emperor Justinian and Empress Theodora. Baklava is also known as the "sweet of a thousand layers."

LEMON MOUSSE

Senator Christopher Bond, MISSOURI

5 eggs, separated
1 cup sugar, divided
2 large lemons, juiced
1 cup heavy cream, whipped
2 teaspoons lemon rind, grated
1 quart berries

In a nonaluminum double boiler, beat egg yolks and ¾ cup of sugar until mixture becomes thick and lemon-colored. Add lemon juice. Cook over simmering water, stirring constantly, until mixture heavily coats the spoon. Caution: Do not allow to boil. Remove from heat; cool. Beat egg whites until stiff and fold into lemon mixture. Fold in whipped cream and lemon rind until mousse is smooth. Chill. Pour berries into a glass serving bowl and sprinkle with remaining sugar. Just before serving, cover berries with mousse.

Makes 8 servings.

This refreshing and simple-to-prepare mousse is equally appealing when served over fresh blueberries, raspberries, blackberries, or strawberries.

Prepare enough for seconds.

CHOCOLATE MELT-AWAY DESSERT

Representative Dan Burton, INDIANA

CRUST:

1	cup flour
¼	cup confectioners' sugar
1	stick margarine
½ to ¾	cup pecans or walnuts, chopped

FILLING:

2	sticks margarine
2	cups confectioners' sugar
4	squares unsweetened chocolate, melted
1	teaspoon vanilla
4	eggs

TOPPING AND GARNISH:

1	8-ounce tub nondairy topping
	Chocolate curls (optional)

To prepare crust, mix together flour, sugar, and margarine. Press into 9- by 13-inch pan. Sprinkle with nuts. Bake 15 minutes in preheated 350-degree oven.

Beat together all filling ingredients except eggs. Add eggs one at a time; beat 10 minutes. Spread over crust. Top with nondairy topping. Chill well. Garnish with chocolate curls, if desired. Cut into squares to serve.

HUNGARIAN RHAPSODY DESSERT

Representative Tom Lantos, CALIFORNIA

CRUST:

    1   cup butter, melted

    ½   cup confectioners' sugar

    2   cups flour

FILLING:

    1½   cups butter or margarine

    1⅓   cups sugar, divided

    8   eggs, separated

    3   teaspoons lemon juice or vanilla extract

    ⅓   cup flour

    2   8-ounce packages cream cheese, softened

To prepare crust, mix melted butter, confectioners' sugar, and flour until blended. Pat into 9- by 13-inch flat ovenproof casserole. Bake for 20 minutes in preheated 350-degree oven.

To prepare filling, cream together butter with 1 cup sugar. Add egg yolks, one at a time, beating well after each addition. Add lemon juice or vanilla. Add flour and cream cheese. Cream until smooth. Whip egg whites, gradually adding remaining ⅓ cup sugar. Fold into egg yolk mixture. Pour into crust. Bake in 350-degree oven 35 to 45 minutes. Dessert is done when knife inserted in thickest part comes out clean. Dust with confectioners' sugar. Cut into small squares. May be frozen.

Makes 18 to 22 servings.

PLUM DUFF

Representative Nancy L. Johnson, CONNECTICUT

2 eggs
½ cup shortening (half margarine, half butter)
1 cup brown sugar, packed
1 cup pitted cooked prunes
1 cup flour
1 teaspoon baking soda
   Pinch of salt
1 tablespoon milk

Beat together eggs, shortening, and sugar until creamed. Stir in prunes. Stir together flour, baking soda, and salt until well blended. Gradually add dry ingredients to creamed mixture. Stir in milk.

Spoon mixture into two greased round 8-inch cake pans. Bake in preheated 375-degree oven for 15 to 20 minutes.

Serve with whipped cream or ice cream.

This recipe is a family favorite given to me by my mother-in-law. It is so popular with my own children that it has become a Christmas tradition.

MEXICAN BANANAS FOSTER

President George W. Bush

10   ounces cajeta (see note)

¼   cup tequila

3   bananas

1   tablespoon butter

1   pint vanilla ice cream or frozen yogurt

¼   cup toasted pecan pieces

Warm cajeta in a microwave oven or in a bowl set over boiling water. Stir in tequila. (Store leftover cajeta in the refrigerator.) Slice bananas in half lengthwise and crosswise. Melt butter and lightly saute bananas in a nonstick skillet, or heat in the microwave.

Put a scoop of vanilla ice cream or frozen yogurt into each bowl. Top with 3 banana quarters. Spoon warm cajeta over bananas to taste. Sprinkle with toasted pecan pieces if desired.

Note: Cajeta, Mexican goat's milk caramel, is sold in jars in the Mexican food section of some supermarkets.

Serves 4.

STRAWBERRY ICE CREAM

Senator Harry Reid, NEVADA

2 pints strawberries
1 cup sugar
1 teaspoon vanilla
1 cup heavy cream
2 cups half-and-half

Puree strawberries in food processor or blender. Add sugar and a little vanilla. Add cream and half-and-half. Freeze mixture in ice cream maker. Serve.

RASPBERRY DELIGHT

★

Senator Gordon Smith, OREGON

CRUST:
- ½ cup margarine, melted
- 1½ cups flour

CREAM CHEESE FILLING:
- 1 8-ounce package cream cheese
- 1 8-ounce tub Cool Whip, thawed
- 1 cup powdered sugar

GLAZE:
- 1¾ cups sugar
- 6 tablespoons cornstarch
- 2 cups water
- 1 small package raspberry jelly powder
- 2 tablespoons butter
- ½ teaspoon almond extract

Mix together margarine and flour and pat in bottom of 9- by 13-inch pan. Bake at 375 degrees for 15 minutes. Cool.

Combine, cream cheese, Cool Whip, and powdered sugar. Blend well. Spread on cooled crust.

To make glaze, mix sugar, cornstarch, water, and jelly powder. Cook until thickened. Remove from heat. Add butter and almond extract.

Cool mixture and spread over cream cheese filling. Chill 6 hours in refrigerator to set. Garnish with whipped cream.

SENATOR PATTY MURRAY'S
APPLE PIE

★

Senator Patty Murray, WASHINGTON

CRUST:

- 3 cups unbleached flour
- 1 teaspoon dry mustard
- ¼ cup sugar
- ½ teaspoon salt
- ½ cup butter
- ⅓ cup vegetable shortening
- ¾ cup sharp cheddar cheese, shredded
- ½ cup cold water

FILLING:

- 9 tart Washington State apples
- ¼ cup unsalted butter, melted
- 1 teaspoon cinnamon
- 2 tablespoons cornstarch
- ½ cup sugar
- 1 teaspoon lemon rind, grated
- 1 teaspoon vanilla

TOPPING:

- 1 teaspoon sugar
- ½ teaspoon cinnamon

For crust combine flour, mustard, sugar, and salt in a mixing bowl. Blend. Using a blender or your fingertips, cut in butter and shortening until the mixture forms small clumps. Then add cheese until dry mixture has coarse clumps.

Preheat oven to 350 degrees. Sprinkle the water, 2 tablespoons at a time, over the mixture and toss with a fork until the dough forms a ball. Knead once or twice in bowl and divide it into slightly unequal halves. Chill dough.

Prepare the filling by coring, halving, and peeling the apples. Cut them into 1-inch chunks. Combine the apples and melted butter in a large bowl. Add the remaining filling ingredients, and toss until apples are evenly coated.

Roll the smaller portion of chilled dough on a floured surface to form a 12-inch circle. Transfer to a 10-inch pie plate, and press into the bottom and sides of the plate. Trim the dough, leaving a 1-inch overhang.

Roll the larger portion of dough out to form a slightly larger circle.

Fill the pie plate with the apple mixture, mounding it slightly. Brush the edge of the bottom crust with water. Move top crust over apples, tucking it under the rim. Trim extra dough, leaving a 1-inch overhang. Seal the edges of the crusts together with a fork and crimp. Trim extra pastry.

Prepare the topping by mixing sugar and cinnamon. Prick top crust in several places with a fork and cut a small vent in center. Brush the top with water, then sprinkle cinnamon sugar. Decorate the top with holiday symbols cut from extra dough.

Bake until filling is bubbling and top is golden, about 1 or 1½ hours.

NATILLAS

★

Senator Pete Domenici, NEW MEXICO

4 eggs, separated
¼ cup flour
1 quart whole milk, divided
¾ cup sugar
⅛ teaspoon salt
Dash of nutmeg

Make paste of egg yolks, flour, and 1 cup milk. Add sugar and salt to remaining milk and scald at medium temperature. Add egg mixture to scalded milk and continue to cook at medium temperature until it reaches consistency of soft custard. Remove from heat and cool to room temperature.

Beat egg whites until stiff, but not dry, and fold into the custard. Chill well before serving. Spoon into individual dishes. Sprinkle with nutmeg and serve.

Makes 6 to 8 servings.

FRENCH SILK PIE

Senator Bob Graham, FLORIDA

CRUST:

    1½ cups butter

    ¾ cup brown sugar

    1½ cups flour

    ½ cup chopped pecans

FILLING:

    ½ pound butter

    1½ cups sugar

    2 teaspoons vanilla

    3 ounces bitter chocolate, melted

    4 eggs

TOPPING:

    2 cups heavy cream

    1 tablespoon instant coffee

    1 tablespoon confectioners' sugar

    ¼ cup sliced almonds, toasted

Melt butter in 9- by 13-inch pan in a 350-degree oven. Add remaining crust ingredients and stir every 5 minutes for 20 minutes, until crisp and crumbly. Do not pat down. Cool.

To make filling, cream butter and sugar. Add vanilla and melted chocolate. Add 2 eggs and beat 3 minutes. Add remaining eggs and beat 3 minutes more. Pour into crust and chill.

Whip cream, adding coffee and confectioners' sugar. Spread over top of pie. Sprinkle with almonds.

Makes 20 servings.

MAPLE APPLE PIE

Senator Jim Jeffords, VERMONT

> 1 9-inch pie crust, unbaked
> 4 apples
> ½ cup maple sugar
> 2 tablespoons butter
> 1 teaspoon cinnamon (optional)
> ⅔ cup cream

Pare and core apples. Cut apples in quarters and arrange on pie crust. Sprinkle generously with maple sugar and dot with butter. Cinnamon may be added to taste. Pour cream over apple mixture. Bake at 450 degrees for 10 minutes. Reduce to 350 degrees and bake until the apples are soft.

This is an old and typical Vermont recipe.

APPLE TART TATIN

Senator Rick Santorum, PENNSYLVANIA

CRUST:

 2½ cups flour

 1 teaspoon salt

 2 teaspoons sugar

 1 cup cold unsalted butter, cubed

 ½ cup cold ice water

TART:

 1½ cups sugar

 8 tablespoons water

 1 cup unsalted butter, cubed

 14 medium apples, cored and quartered

 2 tablespoons sugar

 3 tablespoons cinnamon

 1 teaspoon cloves

First, you need to make your pie crust and chill it in the refrigerator until the apples are ready. Put flour, salt, and sugar in the bowl of a food processor. Add pieces of butter and process until mixture looks like coarse meal. Add the water, a small amount at a time until dough holds together. If dough is crumbly, add a little more water. Put the dough into plastic wrap and store in the refrigerator for at least 1 hour.

Preheat oven to 375 degrees. In a 12-inch cast iron ovenproof skillet, combine sugar and water. Bring to a boil, then cook over medium heat until it turns amber color. Remove from the heat and add the butter.

(Continued)

Arrange the apples decoratively in the skillet on top of the caramelized sugar with the cut side up. Cover the skillet with one layer of apples. Sprinkle apples with half the cinnamon and clove mixture and the 2 tablespoons of sugar.

Add another layer of apples and sprinkle with the remaining cinnamon and clove mixture.

Return the skillet to the stove and cook over low heat for 10 minutes. Be careful not to burn the caramelized sugar. Remove from the heat and let cool.

Roll out the pie crust to a thickness of about ⅛ to ¼ inch and place it over the apples. Trim the edges.

Bake the tart for about 30 to 35 minutes, until the apples are no longer hard, but not mushy. When the crust is golden brown, let cool and place on a platter. Serve warm.

TEXAS PECAN CHOCOLATE CHIP PIE

Senator John Cornyn, TEXAS

1   cup sugar

½   cup flour

2   eggs, beaten

½   cup butter, melted and cooled

1   cup pecans, chopped

1   cup chocolate chips

1   teaspoon vanilla

1   9-inch pie shell, unbaked

Mix sugar and flour. Stir in eggs, butter, pecans, chocolate chips, and vanilla. Pour mixture into an uncooked pie crust and bake for 1 hour at 325 degrees. Cover the edges of the crust with foil to prevent them from becoming too brown.

Pie is done when a toothpick inserted in the middle comes out clean.

Sandy and I often use this recipe. I hope that you will enjoy it as much as we do.

FLUFFY PEANUT BUTTER PIE

★

Senator Lamar Alexander, TENNESSEE

⅓ cup butter

1 cup semisweet chocolate chips

2½ cups crispy rice cereal

1 8-ounce package cream cheese, softened

1 14-ounce can sweetened condensed milk

¾ cup peanut butter

3 tablespoons lemon juice

1 teaspoon vanilla

1 cup heavy whipping cream, whipped

2 teaspoons chocolate syrup

In a heavy saucepan over low heat, melt butter and chocolate chips. Remove from heat. Gently stir in rice cereal until all pieces are completely coated. Press mixture into bottom and sides of a lightly greased 9-inch pie pan. Let chill for 30 minutes.

In a large bowl, beat cream cheese until fluffy. Beat in condensed milk and peanut butter until smooth. Stir in lemon juice and vanilla, then fold in whipped cream.

Pour mixture into pie crust. Drizzle syrup over top of pie; gently swirl with a spoon. Cover and refrigerate pie for 4 hours or until set. Refrigerate leftovers.

> Senator Alexander is a big fan of peanut butter. In fact, when asked about recipes he would want to suggest, his first answer was . . . peanut butter and jelly sandwiches!

VANILLA FUDGE

Representative John Doolittle, CALIFORNIA

2 cups sugar
1 cup heavy cream
¼ cup butter
¼ cup light corn syrup
½ teaspoon salt
1 cup miniature marshmallows
1 tablespoon vanilla
½ cup walnuts or pecans, chopped, optional

Combine sugar, cream, butter, corn syrup, and salt in large, heavy saucepan. Bring to gentle boil over low heat. Cook, stirring constantly, until mixture reaches the soft-ball stage (238 to 240 degrees).

Remove from heat, stirring in marshmallows and vanilla. Stir until candy starts to lose its gloss and marshmallows melt.

Stir in nuts, if desired. Stir until candy starts to set. Do not use mixer. Stir by hand! Pour into buttered 8-inch square pan. Cool.

Makes 25 to 35 pieces.

Note: Do not double the recipe. The fudge becomes too grainy. May be frozen.

CHOCOLATE CHIP CARAMEL BARS

Representative Ron Kind, WISCONSIN

1   18½-ounce package German chocolate cake mix

¾   cup butter, melted

⅔   cup evaporated milk, divided

1   pound caramels, 50 individually wrapped

8   ounces semisweet chocolate chips

Preheat oven to 350 degrees. Lightly grease and flour a 9- by 13-inch pan. In large mixing bowl, combine cake mix, butter, and ⅓ cup evaporated milk. Pat half of mixture into prepared pan. Bake about 10 minutes. Cool.

In a double boiler or microwave-safe bowl in microwave, melt caramels with remaining evaporated milk. Spread over cooled layer in pan. Sprinkle with chocolate chips, then remaining cake mix mixture. Bake 15 minutes until done. Cool.

CHOCOLATE MOUSSE

Representative Nancy Pelosi, CALIFORNIA

1 pound good quality dark chocolate, broken into chunks
8 ounces unsalted butter, cubed
8 eggs whites
4 tablespoons sugar
½ cup heavy cream

In a double boiler, melt chocolate slowly; do not boil. Remove from heat and stir in butter until smooth. Set aside and let cool for 15 minutes.

In separate bowl, beat egg whites and sugar until soft peaks form. Carefully fold egg mixture into chocolate mixture.

In another bowl, beat cream until stiff and then add to mixture. Chill for at least 2 hours.

POTPOURRI

★ 11

Snacks,
Sauces,
and Drinks

RAW CRANBERRY RELISH
A LA NORVEGIENNE

★

Representative Tom Petri, WISCONSIN

1 quart (1 pound) raw cranberries, fresh or frozen
1⅔ to 2 cups sugar
Grated rind of 1 orange

Wash cranberries and place in large bowl with sugar and orange rind. At low speed, take an electric hand mixer and mix for 15 minutes. Let rest 30 minutes then beat again. Continue until the sugar has dissolved completely.

Stir with a wooden spoon for 5 minutes or more and give a vigorous turn for a few minutes whenever you feel like it until sugar dissolves.

It may take a day or two if you are lazy at the stirring.

Store the relish in a jar (preferably a screw-top jar) and the relish will keep for weeks.

This is an old Norwegian recipe. Norwegians use dwarf cranberries, which we call ligonberries. This recipe is an adaptation of the original Norwegian dwarf cranberry recipe.

CRANBERRY-APPLE-PEAR SAUCE

Senator Christopher Bond, Missouri

2 pounds fresh cranberries

4 apples, pared, cored, and diced

3 pears, pared, cored and diced

2 cups golden raisins

2 cups sugar

1 cup fresh orange juice

2½ tablespoons orange rind, grated

2 teaspoons cinnamon

¼ teaspoon freshly grated nutmeg

½ cup plus 2 tablespoons orange-flavored liqueur

Place all ingredients, except liqueur, in a large saucepan. Bring to a boil, then reduce heat. Simmer uncovered 45 minutes, stirring frequently until mixture thickens.

Remove from heat. Stir in liqueur; cool. Refrigerate at least 4 hours. Serve sauce slightly chilled with pork, chicken, or turkey.

Makes 6 cups.

Always included with our Thanksgiving turkey, this festive combination of fruits draws accolades when teamed with a wheel of brie on a holiday buffet table at Christmas.

CORN DODGERS

Representative Porter Goss, FLORIDA

1 cup white cornmeal
1 teaspoon salt
2 cups boiling water
¼ cup milk
1 tablespoon Crisco

Add cornmeal and salt to boiling water. Cook a few minutes until quite thick. Thin with milk to make a paste.

Make into "pone" (oval shape). Grease heavy skillet with Crisco or bacon fat. Place mixture in skillet and bake in 350-degree oven until brown.

BAKED FRUIT

Representative Steny Hoyer, MARYLAND

  1 jar spiced apples
20 ounces sliced peaches
20 ounces pears
20 ounces pineapple chunks
  2 tablespoons flour
½ cup brown sugar, packed
½ cup butter
  1 cup sherry

Drain fruits. Layer fruits in ovenproof casserole dish.

Stir together flour and sugar. Add remaining ingredients and heat until butter melts. Pour over fruit. Refrigerate, covered, overnight. Bake in preheated 350-degree oven for 30 minutes.

FRENCH MINTS

Senator Orrin G. Hatch, UTAH

4   squares unsweetened chocolate
1   cup butter, softened
2   cups confectioners' sugar
4   eggs
1   teaspoon vanilla
1   teaspoon peppermint extract
    Nuts for garnish

Melt chocolate in double boiler over simmering water. Set aside to cool. Using electric beater, beat butter, gradually adding sugar (beat about 15 minutes). Add cooled melted chocolate. Beat 5 minutes more. Beat in eggs, one at a time. Mix in vanilla and peppermint extract. Sprinkle chopped nuts on bottom of 24 paper cupcake liners. Fill half full and sprinkle nuts over top. Freeze mints for at least 3 hours.

Note: Can substitute 6-ounce package of semisweet chocolate chips for sweeter mints.

MARILYN'S MICROWAVE PEANUT BRITTLE

Representative Kay Granger, TEXAS

1 cup sugar
½ cup corn syrup
1 cup raw peanuts
1 teaspoon vanilla
1 tablespoon margarine
1 teaspoon baking soda
Food coloring if desired

In a 2-quart measuring container with handle, stir together sugar, corn syrup, and peanuts (use a wooden spoon, not plastic). Cook 4 minutes on high.

Stir again, then cook another 4 minutes. Add vanilla and margarine. Stir and cook 2 minutes on high. Add baking soda. Stir and pour—fast!! Cool and break into pieces.

My best friend made peanut brittle for us every Christmas. Sometimes her peanut brittle would be delivered in its regular brown sugar color. Other times it would appear dyed red or green. When TCU played football in Ft. Worth and she could attend, she'd deliver it in purple. We would eat so much that she finally began delivering it individually for each of my children and one for me. It just wasn't Christmas without Marilyn's peanut brittle.

Marilyn was always trying to simplify her life (and mine!) so she would use no recipe with more than 5 ingredients. When I pointed out that the peanut brittle violated her rule because it had 6 ingredients, she said the baking soda didn't count because there was so little of it. Try understanding that logic!

UNCLE BEN'S
SPAGHETTI SAUCE

Senator Ben Nelson, NEBRASKA

4	cloves garlic, chopped
3	tablespoons olive oil
1	carrot, chopped
1	stalk celery, chopped
1	onion, chopped
½	green pepper, chopped
	Sausage or meatballs
1½	cups tomato puree
4	ounces tomato paste
¾	cup red wine (not cooking)
10½	ounces beef broth
2	tablespoons lemon rind, chopped
1	teaspoon rosemary
1	teaspoon basil
1	teaspoon oregano

Saute garlic in olive oil, add carrots, celery, onion, and green pepper until lightly colored. Add meats to brown. Add remaining ingredients. Simmer all together, covered, for 2 hours.

Use this sauce as a delicious accompaniment to your favorite pasta dish.

HOMEMADE SALSA

Representative James McCrery, LOUISIANA

3 green onions, chopped
7 medium fresh tomatoes, diced
3 ounces mild green chilies, diced
⅓ cup fresh cilantro, chopped
1½ tablespoons lemon juice, fresh
2 teaspoons soy sauce
⅛ cup salad oil
2 tablespoons red wine vinegar

Combine all ingredients in a large bowl and mix well. Cover and chill overnight. Stores in refrigerator for 1 to 2 weeks. Serve with tortilla chips.

Index by Recipe

Index by Politician

Index by State

About the Author

Linda Bauer has managed to combine several of her favorite interests for *The Great American Sampler Cookbook*—her love of family, reading, education, politics, and writing. She is a native of Ohio and a former Capitol Hill intern, teacher of public, private, and home school students, as well as an educational administrator. She met her husband in Washington, D.C., where he served as a military aide to five presidents. As the wife of an army colonel, Linda has traveled extensively throughout much of the world, which led her to a career as a food and travel columnist for the past twenty years.

Her entire family has enjoyed the exploration of cultures and customs worldwide and each has written and photographed their adventures for their readers. The family currently resides in The Woodlands, Texas, where Linda was recently elected to the Texas State Board of Education, representing 1.4 million people in east Texas.

This book benefits a cause near and dear to her heart—literacy. Proceeds of *The Great American Sampler Cookbook* will be donated to further the cause of literacy in America.